SCUBA DIVING OPERATIONAL RISK MANAGEMENT

An SAS approach to principles, techniques and application

ISBN 978-1-909455-50-4 (Paperback)
ISBN 978-1-909455-51-1 (EPUB ebook)
ISBN 978-1-909455-52-8 (PDF ebook)

Cataloguing-In-Publication Data A catalogue record for this book can be obtained from the British Library.

Published 2024 by

Dived Up Publications
Bournemouth • United Kingdom
Email info@divedup.com
Web DivedUp.com

SCUBA DIVING OPERATIONAL RISK MANAGEMENT

An SAS approach to principles,

techniques and application

Claudio Gino Ferreri

Contents

PART II: PRACTICAL APPLICATION 109

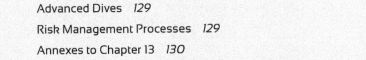

Dedicated to the pilgrims who go below the waves.

We are the pilgrims, master: we shall go
Always a little further: it may be
Beyond the last blue mountain barred with snow.
Across that angry or that glimmering sea,
White on a throne or guarded in a cave
There lives a prophet who can understand
Why men were born: but surely we are brave,
Who take the golden road to Samarkand.

James Elroy Flecker
1884–1915

Publisher's note

The views and opinions in this book are those of the author and not necessarily shared by the publisher. The text is based on the author's knowledge, experience and expertise concerning which the publisher cannot accept responsibility. Readers should draw their own conclusions concerning the possibility of alternative views, accounts, descriptions or explanations.

Preface

It is a humid night somewhere in the South China Sea. A team of SAS assault swimmers are inside the forward chamber of a large diesel electric submarine that is submerged in deep water off the coast. The illumination has been switched to red to allow all eyes to adjust to night vision. The chamber houses a wet mini sub which the assault swimmers are in the process of boarding with their equipment. Once completed, the chamber commences pressurisation and then flooding. Next, the chamber's large hemispherical hatch gradually opens towards the dark water. The mini sub, with the assistance of the submarine's casing divers, slowly makes its way out of the chamber. It is now totally dark. The assault swimmers wear full face masks fitted with an intercom system. They inhale gas from the mini sub's built-in breathing system.

About one hour later the mini sub bottoms-out in shallow water, within swimming distance of the shore. The assault swimmers change over from full face masks to individual half masks and switch breathing apparatus to their personal rebreathers. All of this is performed in total darkness in the cramped confines of the flooded mini sub.

The assault swimmers exit the mini sub and commence the underwater swim to shore. Once there and in a secure location, they change into their land operating equipment for a special reconnaissance operation.

✳

My initial involvement in managing operational diving risks was as a Special Air Service (SAS) Troop Sergeant and Assault Swimmer Class 1 (AS1) in the Australian Army. With about 15 years of experience in SAS Water Operations, I lead teams of highly trained SAS assault swimmers in both surface and underwater activities.

SAS is an unconventional military unit that is trained and organised for operations deep behind enemy lines. Unconventional operations are complex multi-phased activities. They are conducted with minimal resources and backup in order to maintain agility and secrecy. Consequently, to ensure success, considerable pre-planning is carried out. Much of this planning involves the assessment and mitigation of numerous risks.

Recreational divers are to a limited extent in the same situation as the SAS assault swimmer. They conduct dives with the minimum of support and backup. Consequently, the risk management principles and techniques explained in this book are relevant and useful to recreational divers. They are based partly on those used by the SAS and supplemented by the current understanding of the risk management process, as documented by the international risk management standard ISO 31000.

About the Book

This book is primarily for divers using — and organising other divers to use — self-contained underwater breathing apparatus (scuba). By divers I am referring to recreational and technical divers. By scuba I refer not only to open circuit scuba, but also to semi-closed circuit, and closed circuit scuba, commonly known as rebreathers.

Although focusing on recreational scuba, the principles and techniques of risk management covered by the book can be applied to all forms of diving whether they be amateur or professional.

A knowledge and the skill of underwater diving practice, at least to recreational advanced open water level, is required. However, the higher the level of diving knowledge, skill and experience of the user, the more effective will be the application of risk management.

The principles and techniques of risk management in this book are based on two approaches:

- SAS tactical appreciation and planning methodology used for water operations. This methodology is demilitarised and adapted for use by the recreational diver.
- Declassified risk management methodology developed by the US military, initially for aviation quality and reliability applications. This methodology describes procedures for performing failure mode, effects, and criticality analysis (FMECA).

The risk management processes in this book cover the following topics:

- Dive situation analysis.
- Problem identification.
- Deliberate risk management, used for predive risk definition, assessment, and mitigation.
- Immediate risk management, used to manage remaining risk and unexpected events during the execution of a dive.
- Dive planning, used for integrating risk management and the

SMEAC system. This facilitates the creation of comprehensive dive plans and also facilitates the effective delivery of dive briefings.

- Advanced dive planning, used to manage advanced diving practices and tasks, to make them safer and more effective.
- Risk investigation, used for investigating near miss events and incidents associated with all aspects of diving activities.
- Risk monitoring, used for monitoring the execution of diving activities.
- Risk review, used for periodically reviewing all aspects of diving for emerging problems.

The systematic use of risk management principles and techniques enables problems to be clearly defined and consequently should lead to accurately targeted solutions.

Using this Book

This book does not replace traditional methods of managing diving operations. The principles and techniques of risk management outlined in the book may be used, as required, to enhance the effectiveness of traditional diving methodology.

Initial reading of the book should be performed sequentially, that is, from *Chapter 1* through to *Chapter 15*. This is important because each preceding chapter prepares the reader for the following chapter. If the book is not initially read sequentially, it may not make sense.

- Tables are used to assist the reader with the analysis and evaluation process required for risk management.
- Flow charts are used to assist the reader in visualising concepts that are initially explained by narrative.
- Exercises are included to provide opportunities to practice the various risk management techniques. This is the best way to assimilate knowledge and skill.
- Once risk management knowledge and skill have been assimilated the book may subsequently be accessed at any chapter, as required, for refreshment.

If you are an advanced recreational, technical or professional diver, you may consider the situational examples used in the book as too simple for risk management. This has been done deliberately, and for two reasons: First, this book may be used by divers that have recently entered recreational diving, consequently using simple situational examples facilitates their understanding of the principles and techniques. Second, the focus of this book is on diving risk management, not on diving techniques.

Once you understand the principles and techniques of risk management, you can then apply them to your specific category and level of diving whether it be at a basic, advanced, or professional level.

Throughout this book the principles and techniques of risk management are demonstrated by way of examples. When viewing the examples, focus on the *principles* and *techniques* and *not the risk decisions*. Your perception of risk may vary from my perception of risk, consequently, do not become concerned if you do not agree with my risk decisions. There is no right or wrong answer in relation to risk decisions. What is important is that you use the principles and techniques of risk management to arrive at a risk decision that is well thought out, supported by available evidence and that you feel comfortable with. In the end you are responsible for your safety and effectiveness during your dives.

Risk perception is explained in the book. There is also a self-assessment exercise which should give you an indication of your individual perception of risk. This should alleviate any concerns or doubts about variations in risk decisions that may occur. The individual can decide what to accept and reject in the book.

PART I

THEORY

Chapter 1

INTRODUCTION TO RISK MANAGEMENT

Introduction

Scuba diving is an inherently adventurous activity that should be conducted with care. Risk management is a process that can be used in conjunction with dive related resources to reduce the probability of risk and respond to its undesired effects.

This chapter introduces risk management, its modern history and how it is applied situationally. The risk management cycle is broadly outlined to better orientate the reader to the structure of the book. Finally, risk management is described in its various applications to diving.

On completion of this chapter, you should be able to state the following:

- The limitations of dive management by rules.
- The situational approach to risk management.
- The three basic elements of risk.
- The risk management cycle as applied to operational scuba diving.
- The difference between deliberate risk management and immediate risk management.

Historical Perspective

Dive Management by Rules

Historically dive risks have been managed by following long-established rules that are set out in standards, policies, procedure manuals and in some cases legislation. If you operate outside the rules, it is accepted that safety is compromised. The reality however is that the situation is not always the same. The rules may not work in some situations, or worst still, work against you. Also, these rules do not indicate how safe you are in the specific dive situation you are about to experience. Consequently, if you are presented with dive situations that do not fit the model the rules are based on, you then have two choices, either cancel the dive or proceed with the dive not knowing the types of risks you are facing and their risk level.

Since its development in the 1940s, recreational scuba equipment has undergone considerable technical development which continuously challenges established rules. The following timeline shows the changes and their influence on rules:

- 1940s and 1950s — Introduction of the double hose regulator and initial development of safety rules for scuba diving.
- 1960s and 1970s — Introduction of single hose regulator, buoyancy compensators, octopus demand valve and revised safety rules to accommodate these technology changes.
- 1980s — Introduction of dive computers facilitating multi-level diving.
- 1990s — Introduction of technical dive equipment (including rebreathers) and techniques to the general dive community, requiring the development of additional safety rules for extended depth and dive duration.
- 2000 to present — Introduction of solo diving techniques and associated rules to the recreational diving community.

Rules are still important as a baseline for safe diving. However, by assessing the situational parameters such as the specific dive conditions, the dive activity and diver capability, the safety of the dive and its successful outcome can be enhanced to an optimum level.

Origins of Modern Risk Management

The principles and techniques of risk management, as applied in recent decades, were originally developed in Germany during the Second World War. They were used to optimise the reliability of military aircraft production processes. In the late 1940s these principles and techniques were transferred to the US military where they were applied to the development of military aviation and later to aerospace applications. The first draft by the US military was MIL-STD-1629 *Procedures for Performing a Failure Mode, Effects and Criticality Analysis* (1949), abbreviated as FMECA.

Over the decades this standard was adopted and modified by various manufacturing and service industries for their specific application. Notable civilian and government agencies using versions of FMECA are NASA and the Ford Motor Company. Consequently, some countries developed their own standards, for example the UK with BS 5760-5:1991 (FMEA and FMECA).

In 1995 the Australia/New Zealand risk management standard was developed as AS/NZ 4360:1995 by Standards Australia. This standard acknowledges and describes the principles and techniques of FMECA for general purpose risk management application and also introduces the risk management process. In 2009 the International Organisation for Standards, published ISO 31000:2009, based on the AS/NZ 4360 risk management standard. At the time of writing, the current risk management standard is ISO 31000:2018.

The declassified standards guideline referred to in this book is the later edition MIL-STD-1629A *Procedures for Performing a Failure Mode, Effects and Criticality Analysis* (24 November 1980). This version is used because the terminology "cause", "event" and "effect" in the standard can be applied to risk investigations, as discussed in a later chapter of the book. This enables a consistent approach to risk management and avoids confusion with terminology.

Situational Approach

Risks associated with scuba diving are diverse depending on the various situational parameters. It therefore becomes apparent that some analysis is required to adapt existing rules to varying dive sites and their associated conditions.

The situational approach to managing dive related risks requires that five basic elements be considered, as follows:

- The specific dive site.
- The conditions at the dive site.
- The dive activity and its phases at the dive site.
- Diver capability.
- The problems that may occur during the dive activity that represent a risk to the diver and/or the successful outcome of the dive.

The interaction of the five elements and the resulting problems and risk is shown at Figure 1.1.

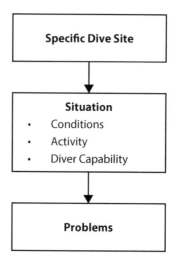

Figure 1.1. Situational approach

Problem

According to the *Oxford English Dictionary* a problem is "a thing that is difficult to deal with or to understand." Consequently, problems result from uncertainty as shown at Figure 1.2.

A problem can be compared to an onion, with many layers of uncertainty that need to be peeled back in order to define and solve it. Uncertainty about a problem may lead to haphazard solutions that may not resolve it, or in some situations make it worse.

The structured assessment of significant problems by risk management reduces uncertainty and leads to solutions that accurately target the problem as shown at Figure 1.3.

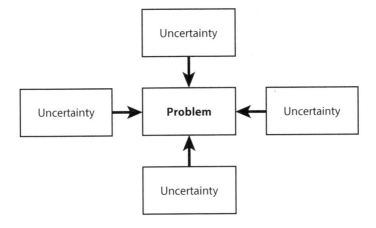

Figure 1.2. Problem

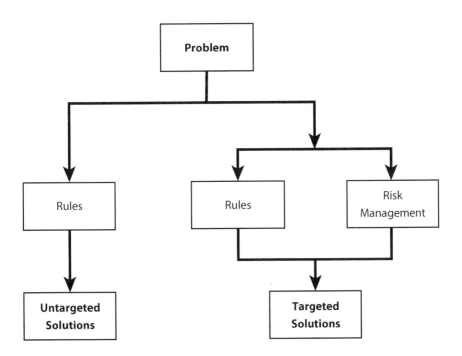

Figure 1.3. Structure of risk

Diving Risk Management Cycle

The risk management cycle, shown in Figure 1.4, is the process that is described in this book to manage risk associated with scuba diving activity. This cycle broadly aligns with the risk management process originally described by AS/NZ 4360 in 1995 and later by ISO 31000.

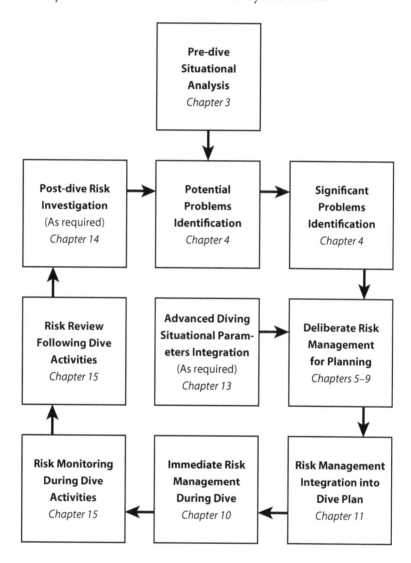

Figure 1.4. Risk management cycle

Application of the Diving Risk Management Cycle

Risk management applied from a situational perspective in relation to existing conditions, specific dive activity and diver capability can deliver outcomes as shown at Table 1.5 below.

Stages of the Risk Management Cycle	Process Outcomes	Book Chapter
Define the situation	• Describe the situation of the proposed dive • Identify the phases of the proposed dive activity	3
Identify dive related problems	• Identify potential problems related to proposed dive • From the potential problem list related to a proposed dive, identify the significant problems	4
Identify and define the risk	• Identify the risk presented by the significant problems • Identify the cause, event and effects related to the risks	5
Existing risk mitigation	• Identify existing risk mitigation to manage the risks, relative to causes and effects • Assess the adequacy of existing risk mitigation	6
Risk analysis	• Measure the risk level from the perspective of probability of event and severity of effect	7
Risk evaluation	• Evaluate the risk for acceptability	8
Additional risk mitigation	• If the risk level is not acceptable, identify additional risk mitigation • Assess the effectiveness, practicality, and cost effectiveness of the additional risk mitigation • Assess the adequacy of additional risk mitigation • Measure the additional mitigated risk level from the perspective of probability and effect • Evaluate the acceptability of the treated risk based on the treated risk level	9

Table 1.5. Application of the risk management cycle

Deliberate Risk Management

Deliberate risk management is used during the planning of dives, associated with situational parameters, to reduce risk to a level that is as low as reasonably practicable and acceptable. In application, deliberate risk management can be applied at various levels, as discussed in Chapter 2.

Immediate Risk Management

Immediate risk management is used during the conduct of dives to manage the residual risk that remains following deliberate risk management and planning. It is also used for unidentified risks that may present during a dive.

Techniques for immediate risk management are as follows:
- Using past experience and planning.
- Situational awareness.
- Quick decision process.

Techniques of immediate risk management are explained in greater detail in Chapter 10.

Risk Register

A Risk Register is a document used to record the outcome of the various processes, information gathering, decision-making and outcomes fundamental to diving risk management. During the course of the book, numerous examples are given of the kind of entries that should be entered into a Risk Register.

Risk Management Exercises

Risk management exercises have been developed for many chapters so that you can practice and better assimilate the principles and techniques covered. There is no right or wrong answer as your perception of risk may vary from mine. A Risk Register is included in Chapter 12, Risk Management Toolkit, so that you may compare the results.

The risk management exercises are as follows:

Chapter	Exercise
2	Personal Risk Perception Assessment
3	Situation Report
4	Identify Dive Related Problems
5	Identify and Describe the Risk
6	Determine Existing Risk Mitigation
7	Risk Analysis
8	Risk Evaluation
9	Additional Risk Mitigation
10	Immediate Risk Management
12	Entering Risk Data in the Risk Register
12	Dive Plan
13	Advanced Diving Situational Parameters
14	Risk Investigation
15	Risk Review

Table 1.6. Risk management exercises

Chapter 2 — Deliberate Risk Management

Chapter 2 will introduce the *deliberate risk management process* for managing risks and associated with the planning of dive activities.

DELIBERATE RISK MANAGEMENT

Introduction

Deliberate risk management, as the name suggests, is a planned, methodical, and calculated approach to managing risk. It involves gathering situational information, analysis, evaluation, and formation of measures to mitigate identified risks.

Deliberate risk management, as explained in this chapter, is partly based on SAS methodology, as well as methodology described in MIL-STD-1629A *Procedures for Performing a Failure Mode, Effects and Criticality Analysis* (24 November 1980).

This chapter introduces the various levels and applications in which deliberate risk management can be used. In addition, the reader is introduced to the decision benchmarks that are used in the various stages of the process. Finally, risk perception is discussed, and an exercise is included so the reader can better understand how risk perception influences risk decisions.

On completion of this chapter, you should be able to identify:

- The four applications of deliberate risk management.
- The five levels of deliberate risk management.
- The ten factors of risk perception.
- Your own level of risk perception.

Application of Deliberate Risk Management

These principles and techniques can be used for planning dives and as a basis for investigating near miss events and incidents.

Deliberate Risk Management for Planning

As a planning tool, deliberate risk management is used for managing foreseeable risks before diving activities commence. Applications for deliberate risk management in planning are as follows:

- Dive planning.
- Task planning.
- Deep dive planning.
- Rebreather dive planning.

Application Levels for Dive Planning

Risk management can be applied sequentially at various levels based on the degree of uncertainty surrounding a prospective dive. If you are diving in a location that is very familiar, where conditions are predictable and the activity is well practiced, the application of risk management will range from nil required to minimal, for example, potential problem identification.

However, if you are diving in a location that is unfamiliar, where conditions are unknown, changeable, or uncertain and activity procedures indeterminate, then a more comprehensive risk management approach is required to identify significant problems and solutions. The levels of deliberate risk management application can be classified as shown at Table 2.1.

Examples of diving scenarios and associated risk management implementation levels are shown at Table 2.2.

Chapters 3 to 9 will explain the process of deliberate risk management in greater detail.

Chapter 12 introduces you to the Risk Management Toolkit which can be used for the different levels of deliberate risk management.

Risk Management Application Level	Risk Management Activity	Outcome	Risk Management Action
RM Level 1	Identify potential problems	No potential problems found	No further action required, proceed cautiously with dive
		Potential problems found	Move to Level 2
RM Level 2	Identify significant problems	No significant problems found	No further action required, proceed cautiously with dive
		Significant problems found	Move to Level 3
RM Level 3	Identify and define the risk and determine adequacy of existing risk mitigation	Existing risk mitigation adequate for all risks	No further action required, proceed cautiously with dive
		One or all existing risk mitigations not adequate for one or all risks	Move to Level 4
RM Level 4	Assess risk	Risk level acceptable for all identified risks	No further action required, proceed cautiously with dive
		Risk level for one or more risks is not acceptable	Move to Level 5
RM Level 5	Implement additional risk mitigation	Risk level acceptable for all mitigated risks	No further action required, proceed cautiously with dive
		Risk level not acceptable for one or more mitigated risks	Consider cancelling dive

Table 2.1. Deliberate risk management application levels

	Diving Scenarios		
	Shallow Recreational Dive to 10 metres	**Deep Recreational Dive to 40 metres**	**Technical Dive to 60 metres**
Risk Management Level	Simple situation in relation to conditions, activity, and diver capability.	Complex situation in relation to conditions, activity, and diver capability.	Very complex situation in relation to conditions, activity, and diver capability.
RM Level 1 Identify potential problems	No potential problems identified. Dive may proceed with caution.	3 x potential problems identified. Move to RM Level 2.	10 x potential problems identified. Move to RM Level 2.
RM Level 2 Identify significant problems		2 x significant problems identified. Move to RM Level 3.	4 x significant problems identified. Move to RM Level 3.
RM Level 3 Identify and define risks and determine adequacy of existing risk mitigation		2 x risk defined. Some existing risk mitigation inadequate. Move to RM Level 4.	4 x risks defined. Some existing risk mitigation inadequate. Move to RM Level 4.
RM Level 4 Assess risks		1 x risk assessed as a low risk and acceptable. 1 x risk assessed as a medium risk and unacceptable. Move to RM Level 5.	2 x risks assessed as a low risk and acceptable. 1 x risk assessed as a medium risk and acceptable. 1 x risk assessed as a high risk and not acceptable. Move to RM Level 5.
RM Level 5 Implement additional risk mitigation		1 x medium risk mitigated and re-assessed as a low risk and acceptable. Dive may proceed with caution.	1 x high risk mitigated and re-assessed as a medium risk and acceptable. Dive may proceed with caution.

Table 2.2. Examples of deliberate risk
management scenario application

Deliberate Risk Management for Investigations

As an investigative tool, deliberate risk management may be applied after dive activities have occurred and problems have been detected. These problems may be near miss events and incidents. Applications of deliberate risk management for investigations are as follows:

- Dive procedure review.
- Post incident investigation.
- Task failure investigation.
- Dive equipment failure investigation.

It is important at this point to note the difference between a near miss, an incident, and an accident:

- A near miss event is a risk related event that results in no damage, injury, or loss of life.
- An incident is a risk related event that results in no serious damage, injury, or loss of life.
- An accident is a risk related event that results in serious damage, injury, or loss of life.

Near miss events and incidents may be investigated by the individual or team as no serious damage, injury or loss of life has occurred. Accident investigations are conducted by government agencies. Due to the seriousness and complexity of the event and subsequent effect, accident investigations are beyond the capability of the lay person.

Expectations of Deliberate Risk Management

Deliberate risk management should reduce uncertainty and delivers the following benefits:

- Risks are clearly defined.
- Existing risk mitigation is assessed for relevancy, accuracy, effectiveness and adequacy.
- The level of risk is measured.
- The risk is further mitigated.
- Risks are monitored.
- Risks can be reviewed.

- The risk is communicated to others in a logical and meaningful way.

Deliberate Risk Management Decision Benchmarks

In order to conduct the various stages of risk management, decision benchmarks are required so that critical decisions are made in a manner that is systematic and consistent. The following is a list of decision benchmarks used in the process:

- Existing risk mitigation adequacy table.
- Risk probability table.
- Risk severity table.
- Risk level analysis table.
- Risk evaluation table.
- Additional risk mitigation adequacy table.

To facilitate the explanation of the deliberate risk management process, in the following chapters I have developed risk management decision benchmarks specific to operational scuba dive related risk management.

Limitations of Deliberate Risk Management

Activity and Risk

If a dive activity is conducted, risk management may reduce the risk but will not completely remove it. There will always be a remaining risk which may or may not be acceptable. The only way to completely remove the risk is to cancel the dive activity.

Risk Perception

Perception of risk varies between individuals, driven by the following factors:

- Personal experience, for example, an experienced diver will be more accepting of risk than an inexperienced diver.
- Perceived extremity of event, for example, an event that has catastrophic consequences may create a bias towards avoiding the activity.
- Perceived probability of event, for example, bias towards denying the possibility of suffering decompression sickness on repetitive dives.

- Recognition, for example, failing to recognise risk indicators from near miss events.
- Degree of control, for example, perceived ability or inability to control challenging dives.
- Dread and fear, for example, unreasonable or illogical fear of environmental conditions or certain marine life.
- Proximity of impact, for example, diving in areas where catastrophic events have recently occurred (drowning, shark attack, etc.).
- Cueing, for example, adverse and/or exaggerated media reporting of risks.
- Beliefs, emotions and values, for example, being naturally risk averse or risk taking.
- Complacency, for example, experienced divers foregoing critical safety checks which may result in an adverse event.

Perception Over Time

Over time the perception of the diver will change, thereby affecting decisions. On completion of initial training they will tend to be risk averse, due to lack of experience. However, after completing a number of dives confidence will improve. During this period, the diver may tend to become overconfident and dangerously risk accepting. As their diving continues they may experience a number of near miss events, combined with a few incidents. Eventually, the diver develops an attitude of risk aversion balanced with the occasional stint of risk acceptance, when appropriate.

Risk Perception and Risk Management

Risk perception influences the risk management process in the following ways:
- Suitability of decision criteria/benchmarks.
- Existence of dive related problems.
- Translation of problems into risks.
- Adequacy of existing risk mitigation.
- Level of risk that a problem presents.
- Selection of measures to mitigate the risk.
- Aborting a commenced dive.
- Decision to proceed with the dive or cancel the dive.

Managing Risk Perception

Risk perception can be managed in the following ways:

- Recognising the existence of bias caused by perception.
- When operating in dive teams, conferring with others on risk management in order to achieve a more balanced perception.
- Considering the weakest members of a team when evaluating risks.
- If uncertainty still exists, at conclusion of the risk management process, considering whether to err on the side of safety.
- Avoiding quick solutions as they may not accurately target the true cause of the risk.

Understanding risk perception by the individual or groups and using a structured and rigorous risk management approach should result in consistent and valid risk decisions that accurately target the problem.

Perception of Risk Terminology

Some readers may be more familiar with other risk terms. Consequently, to facilitate interpretation of risk terminology used in this book, a list comparing various terms is shown at Table 2.3.

Risk terms used in this book	Other comparable risk terms (approximate)
Situation	Context, Circumstances, Status
Risk	Hazard, Threat
Cause	Source, Root, Trigger
Event	Incident, Occurrence, Issue, Problem, Failure mode
Effect	Consequences, Impact, Outcome, Cost, Harm
Probability	Likelihood, Frequency, Chance, Odds
Severity	Magnitude
Mitigation	Controls, Safety measures, Safety management, Treatment, Contingency
Significant	Substantial, Considerable, Critical
Objective	Goal, Purpose
Benchmarks	Criteria, Measures, Conditions, Standards
Risk Level	Criticality

Table 2.3. Risk terminology comparison

Perception of Occurrence

The term "probability" is used in this book. In this application, probability is based on the analysis of situational parameters and the individual's perception of risk. It is used for predicting the probability of future events. Other comparable perceptions of occurrence terms that some readers may be more familiar with are shown at Table 2.4. Decompression sickness (DCS) is used as the event example. The figures are not based on actual data, they are purely illustrative.

Term	Application	Narrative Expression	Mathematical Expression
Likelihood	Qualitative	Rare probability of DCS event	n/a
Frequency	Quantitative	50 DCS events per 10,000 dives per year	50/10,000 per year
Probability	Quantitative	50 DCS events per 10,000 dives	0.005 or 0.5% probability
Chance	Quantitative	One in two hundred chances of DCS event	1/200
Odds	Quantitative	DCS event odds are one in 200	1/200

Table 2.4. Chance of occurrence terms

Qualitative and Quantitative Analysis

Risk management outlined in this handbook is based on a qualitative analysis of situational parameters. The analysis is dependent on the individual's risk perception, based on diving knowledge, skill and experience. The resulting risk management decision can best be described as an *educated hypothesis*. Qualitative analysis tends to be *subjective* in application as it is based on perception.

Qualitative analysis can be made semi-quantitative by allocating numerical scales to narrative statements in order to arrive at a more granular risk management decision. Risk analysis techniques are explained in Chapter 7.

Quantitative analysis in diving is applied to the study of near misses, incidents and accidents over a period of time or number of dives. It produces numbers which can then be used to mathematically calculate patterns or trends. It tests the hypothesis generated by qualitative analysis. Quantitative analysis tends to be *objective* in application. The limitation of quantitative analysis, when applied to past incidents, is that it may not accurately predict future events.

Exercise — Personal Risk Perception Assessment

Assess yourself against the perception parameters using the susceptibility scale at Table 2.5.

Risk Perception Descriptor	Risk Perception Level				
	Strongly Disagree 1	Moderately Disagree 2	Neutral 3	Moderately Agree 4	Strongly Agree 5
Personal experience Rebreathers are extremely dangerous					
Perceived extremity of event I have stopped diving altogether because a close friend died scuba diving					
Perceived probability of event I always do a safety stop regardless of depth of dive					
Recognition I will cancel the dive if my regulator second stage has a small bubble leak					
Degree of control I do not like diving anywhere there are currents					
Beliefs, emotions and values I do not like diving alone					
Proximity of impact I am not diving where a shark attacked a diver last week					
Cueing News media claim that cave diving is extremely dangerous					
Dread and fear I am very scared of night dives					
Complacency I always check my buddy before entering the water					

Table 2.5. Personal perception susceptibility and reliability assessment

Place the number from the Risk Perception Level in the box that you believe best describes your agreement level in relation to each Risk Perception Descriptor. Table 2.5 is also available to download from www.DivedUp.com/diving-risk-management-templates/

Scoring

Add up all the numbers in the boxes and compare your score to the risk perception rating at Table 2.6.

Risk Perception Score	Risk Perception Rating
10 to 20	Risk accepting
21 to 39	Risk accepting in some situations
40 to 50	Risk averse

Table 2.6. Risk perception rating

There is no right or wrong answer as we all vary in our individual perception of risk. Your risk perception will also change over time. Consequently, if you repeat the assessment after a considerable period of time, number of dives and/or additional training, you may notice a change in perception.

Chapter 3 — Define the Situation

Chapter 3 will explain how to *define the situation* for the dive and subsequently produce a Situation Report.

DEFINE THE SITUATION

Introduction

The process for defining the situation is based on SAS tactical appreciation methodology, also known as *situational analysis*. As part of preliminary planning the SAS planner uses situational analysis to conduct a detailed investigation of the area in which they intend to conduct operations.

The recreational diver can make use of situational analysis to investigate the dive site, in particular if it is a new dive site or one that has changing environmental conditions that may significantly affect the safety of the dive.

As a precursor to situational analysis, this chapter explains how to identify and describe the three main situational components which establish the context of the dive. This is an important step which needs to be done before starting the risk management process.

On completion of this chapter, you should be able to produce a Situation Report for a proposed dive.

Situational Parameters of the Dive

The context of a dive consists of three main situational parameters as follows:
- Dive conditions — outlines the who, what, where, when, how and why.
- Dive activity — which consists of the various phases of the dive.
- Diver capability — the skill, knowledge and experience of the participants.

The combination of dive conditions, activity and diver capability results in the production of a Situation Report which is used for risk management.

In Chapter 13, additional situational parameters which are considered when planning more advanced dives will be explained.

Importance of Understanding the Situation

The risk management process and its outcomes are dependent on understanding the situation, which:
- Enables identification of risk, its causes, the event and effect(s).
- Enables identification of existing risk mitigation.
- Facilitates the assessment and evaluation of risk.
- Facilitates the development of additional risk mitigation, as required.

If the risk management process is undertaken without a clear understanding of the situation, risks, subsequent assessments and additional risk mitigation are just a guessing process which results in untargeted solutions.

Dive Conditions Parameters

The situation outlines the conditional parameters of the dive. Each dive is defined by the following parameters:
- Background.
- Mission.
- Outcomes.
- General Outline.
- Underwater Tasks.
- Date/time limitations.
- Environment of the dive activity.
- Equipment to be used.

Background
This provides background information and answers the question of *why* we are planning the dive. The following are examples of dives that may be planned:
- Exploration.
- Object recovery.
- Fish hunting.
- Bottom survey.
- Underwater photography.

- Wreck exploration.
- Deep dive.
- Night dive.
- Decompression dive.
- Cave dive.

Background should be expressed in a paragraph containing the following:
- Location of proposed activity.
- Brief description of location.
- Key outcomes of the activity.

Mission

The mission is a brief statement of what is to be achieved, for example, "Explore the shipwreck HMAS *Swan* which is in 30 metres of water one mile west of Dunsborough". Should be expressed in one or two sentences.

Outcomes

The outcomes are the desired result of the dive, for example, "Penetrate and explore all the compartments of the wreck." Outcomes may be single or multiple.

General Outline

This is the plan of what is going to occur and how many dives will be executed. It may be expressed in a paragraph.

Underwater Tasks

This is a detailed plan for any specific tasks that may be performed during the dive and outcomes desired. For casual dives this may be omitted. The plan is divided into phases, each covering a particular stage of the task and it should include the following information:
- Type of underwater task.
- Task objective.
- Task phases.
- Task phase requirements.
- Team composition.

Date/Time Limitations

This sets the start and finish of the dive which may be conducted in a single day with a single dive, or over several weeks with multiple dives each day.

- Time may be linked to tidal information when tidal ranges are large and/or currents are significant.
- Tides may dictate when it is safe to dive.

Environment of the Dive Activity

The environment consists of the following main elements:

- Atmosphere.
- Water.
- Underwater Terrain.
- Day/night.

The relationship between the main elements of the environment and their respective sub-elements are shown at Table 3.1.

Main Elements	Atmosphere	Water	Underwater Terrain Composition	Underwater Terrain Configuration
	Air temperature	Water temperature	Sand	Caves
	Air visibility	Water visibility	Mud	Cavern
	Wind strength	Current strength	Shale	Walls
	Wind direction	Current direction	Rock	Slopes
		Sea State	Coral	Mounts
Sub-elements		Tide level	Seaweed	Gutters
		Tidal flow	Gravel	Chasms
			Silt	Abysses
				Channel
				River
				Sinkhole

Table 3.1. Environmental elements

Equipment to be Used

Dive equipment can be classified under the following main categories:

- Vision.
- Life support.
- Buoyancy control.
- Propulsion.
- Thermal protection.
- Time/depth monitoring.
- Navigation.
- Safety/emergency.
- Tools.
- Communication.

Dive equipment is critical to the safety of the diver. The selection of specific items within each category will vary with water temperature, currents, depth, duration of dive and underwater visibility.

Dive Activity Parameters

Type of Dive

Dives can be grouped into the following main deployment categories:

- Shore Dive.
- Boat Dive.

Each dive type can be further broken down into activity phases, as follows:

Boat dive general outline

- Loading boat.
- Boat passage.
- Dressing for the dive.
- Water entry.
- Descent to bottom.
- Activity on bottom.
- Ascent to surface.
- Water exit.

- Post dive activity.
- Unloading boat.

Shore dive general outline
- Dressing for dive.
- Shore water entry.
- Swim to water descent point.
- Descent to bottom.
- Activity on bottom.
- Ascent to surface.
- Swim back to shore exit point.
- Shore water exit.
- Post dive activity.

Diver Capability Parameters

The qualification, experience and fitness of the divers will have considerable influence on the management of risk. It will also enable unforeseen risks to be controlled in situ during the dive through situational awareness, previous experience, and stress control.

The capability of a diver can be determined from the following perspectives:
- Diver qualification.
- Diver experience.
- Diver fitness.

Qualification and Experience
The range of diver qualification levels in relation to operational depth are shown at Table 3.2. They are based on parameters established by recreational diving training agencies. They may vary slightly between different agencies and over time.

Diver Type	Diver Qualification	Maximum Operational Depth
Recreational Diver	Open Water Diver	18 metres
	Advanced Open Water Diver	30 metres
	Deep Diver	40 metres
Technical Diver	Decompression Diver	45 metres
	Trimix Diver	60 metres
	Advanced Trimix Diver	90 metres

Table 3.2. Diver qualification and depth

Diver experience is important for managing residual risk and unexpected events during the conduct of dives. The list shown at Table 3.3 outlines the amount of experience that is desirable, as a minimum, before progressing to the next level of training.

Qualifications	Course Experience	Additional Experience	Maximum Operational Depth
Open Water Diver	4 dives	20 dives	18 metres
Advanced Open Water	4 dives	20 dives	30 metres
Deep Diver	3 dives		40 metres

Table 3.3. Diver experience

Fitness

Diver fitness is important. Individuals need to be fit to dive. Professional divers, that is, military and commercial divers, are required to undergo a diving medical examination at least once every twelve months. In some cases, additional medical checks are conducted immediately before diving operations commence. In recreational diving situations, it is accepted that it is the responsibility of the individual diver to ensure that they are fit to dive.

Information Sources

Information sources related to diver capability are outlined in Table 3.4.

Diver Capability Parameter	Information Source
Diver medical fitness	Dive medical report
Diver knowledge and skill	Dive qualification
Diver experience	Dive log

Table 3.4. Diver capability information sources

Diver Capability and Challenging Dive Conditions

Challenging dives can be characterised as those involving:

- Deep water.
- Limited underwater visibility.
- Water current.
- Low water temperature.
- Complex dive equipment configuration.
- Large wrecks.
- Caves and caverns.
- Underwater tasks.

The problems that may arise as a result of challenging conditions and diver capability are shown at Table 3.5.

Challenging Dive Condition	Potential Problems	Relevant Diver Capabilities
Deep water	• Nitrogen narcosis susceptibility • Decompression sickness susceptibility • Oxygen poisoning susceptibility • Disorientation in midwater	Diver fitness Diver knowledge Diver skill Diver experience
Limited underwater visibility	• Diver separation • Inability to navigate in low visibility	
Water current	• Diver fatigue swimming against current	
Low water temperature	• Hypothermia susceptibility	
Complex dive equipment configuration	• Equipment entanglement • Poor buoyancy control • Inability to access part of equipment • Inability to enter/exit water	

Table 3.5. Problem identification

Situation Report: Shipwreck Dive Example

Introduction

The following is an example of a completed situation document for a shipwreck dive. It displays the type of information required before a risk management process can commence.

Background

Over the last year we have considered a dive on the wreck of the HMAS *Swan* located at Dunsborough on the southwestern coast of Western Australia, about 200 kilometres south of Perth. The wreck is a former Royal Australian Navy River Class Destroyer Escort that was scuttled at the end of 1997 about 1.3 nautical miles from Meelup Beach near Dunsborough. The shipwreck lies on a sandy bottom at 31 metres depth. The shipwreck is made safe for recreational diving with numerous openings cut in the side of the hull for emergency egress. See illustration of *Swan* wreck at Figure 3.6.

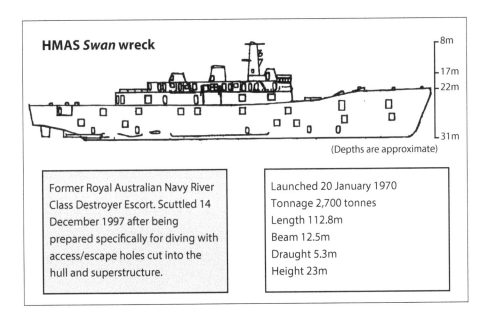

Figure 3.6. Starboard side view of HMAS *Swan* wreck

Mission
The mission is to conduct two dives on the wreck of HMAS *Swan*.

Outcomes
The objective is to explore the wreck as a recreational pursuit.

General Outline
The dive is to be executed in the following phases:
- Phase 1 — Load dive boat at Busselton Geographe Bay Marina and motor to wreck dive position.
- Phase 2 — Execute dive one.
- Phase 3 — Surface interval.
- Phase 4 — Execute dive two.
- Phase 5 — Motor back to marina and unload boat.

Underwater Tasks
Omitted as this is a simple dive and no specific tasks are to be performed.

Date/Time Limitations
The two dives are to be completed. Projected time schedule is as follows:
- Phase 1 — 0900 to 1000 hrs.
- Phase 2 — 1030 to 1130 hrs.
- Phase 3 — 1130 to 1300 hrs.
- Phase 4 — 1300 to 1400 hrs.
- Phase 5 — 1400 to 1530 hrs.

Planned dive time for each dive is 60 minutes.

Environment of Dive Activity
Environment of the dive activity is determined as shown at Table 3.7.

Atmosphere		Water		Underwater Terrain Yes or No	
Air temperature	24C	Temperature	20C	Sand	Yes
Air visibility	Clear	Visibility	20m	Mud	No
Wind strength	5knts	Current strength	nil	Shale	No
Wind direction	SW	Current direction	n/a	Rock	No
		Sea state	Calm	Coral	No
		Tide level	1m	Seaweed	No
		Tidal flow	nil	Caves	No
				Walls	No
				Slopes	No
				Mounts	No
				Gutters	No
				Chasms	No
				Abysses	No
				Wreck	Yes

Table 3.7. Environment of dive

Equipment to be Used

Equipment to be used is shown at Table 3.8.

Equipment Category	Specific Equipment Type	Required Yes or No
Thermal protection	5mm wetsuit	Yes
Propulsion	Fins	Yes
Life support	Normal regulator with octopus second stage and gas contents gauge	Yes
Buoyancy control	Buoyancy compensator and weights	Yes
Vision	Mask	Yes
Communication	Hand signals	Yes
Time/depth monitoring	Dive computer	Yes
Navigation	Compass	Yes
Safety equipment	Surface marker buoy, spool and line; snorkel	Yes
Tools	Knife	Yes

Table 3.8. Equipment to be used

Dive Activity

Boat dive activity general outline:

- Loading boat — at Meelup Beach.
- Boat passage — about 10 Minutes to wreck site.
- Dressing for the dive — on boat at wreck site.
- Water entry — via starboard side of boat.
- Descent to bottom — via mooring line from surface to top of wreck superstructure.
- Activity on bottom — explore wreck starting from keel and gradually working up to top of superstructure.
- Ascent to surface — from top of superstructure ascend to safety stop via mooring line. Complete safety stop and then ascend to surface.
- Water exit — via starboard side of boat.
- Post dive activity — diver check, secure dive equipment.
- Unloading boat — at Meelup Beach.

Dive Team Composition

Dive team composition is as follows:

- Ten divers.
- All are qualified to Advanced Open Water level.
- Each diver has completed over 100 open water dives.
- All have completed dives within the last three months.

Exercise — Situation Report

Using the information from Chapter 3 develop a Situation Report for a significant dive you are planning in the near future. You may find the template at *page 114* useful.

Chapter 4 — Identify Dive Related Problems

Chapter 4 will explain how to identify dive related problems using the *Problem Identification Checklist.*

IDENTIFY DIVE RELATED PROBLEMS

Introduction

Identification of problems is a methodology that is used by the military, including the SAS, to quickly identify what can go wrong on a future operation that is being planned. The technique used is called "What-if." That is, during each phase of the operation, *what-if* something happens?

The recreational diver can use the same technique during the initial planning of a dive activity by first dividing it into separate phases. This facilitates the execution, planning and allocation of administrative and logistic resources to the various phases of the dive activity and the quick identification of potential problems. This chapter explains how dive related problems are identified. This is an important precursor to risk identification and definition.

On completion of this chapter, you should be able to:

- Identify potential dive related problems.
- Determine if the identified potential problems are significant and consequently require further risk management.

Problem Identification

Problems are undesirable events which may be perceived and subsequently expressed by the individual in any of the following ways:

- Event, incident, happening, episode, experience, encounter, occurrence. For example: experience narcosis; encounter an aggressive shark.
- Accident, mishap, catastrophe, disaster, mistake. For example: forget to turn on the gas cylinder hand valve; burst low pressure hose.
- Result, consequence, outcome, objective. For example: run out of breathing gas; unable to complete safety stop.

Potential Problems

Immediate Analysis (what-if)

A potential problem is a problem whose occurrence may be considered *possible*. The process is conducted in an immediate manner using judgement based on experience and without the support of evidence. The technique involves asking the question "what-if" for each dive activity. This enables quick progress through a problem identification checklist, identifying obvious potential problems, analogous to separating wheat from chaff. Potential problem criteria are shown at Table 4.1.

Benchmarks	Descriptor
Occurrence	Possibility of occurrence is perceived to exist based on experience without the support of evidence
Outcome	Possibility that it may lead to serious harm or fatality to the diver and/or failure of task
Lack of mitigation	Measures to mitigate the problem are unknown

Table 4.1. Potential problems

Potential problems are identified by reference to the problem identification checklist for an immediate analysis. The checklist tables included in this book have been designed for two general dive activities:
- Shore dive.
- Boat dive.

Immediate analysis using a problem identification checklist has two main objectives:
- Quick identification of potential problems.
- Reducing the chance of missing problems that may subsequently be significant to the dive.

The immediate analysis process is shown at Figure 4.2.

The boat dive problem identification checklist and shore dive problem identification checklist templates are provided in the Risk Management Toolkit at *page 116.*

These checklists are not to be considered complete, as problems additional to those on the checklists may be identified, in particular if advanced dives are conducted involving tasks, increased depth and/or the use of rebreathers (such Advanced Diving Situational Parameters are discussed in Chapter 13).

The problems identified are potential problems and may need to be further analysed to determine if they are *significant*.

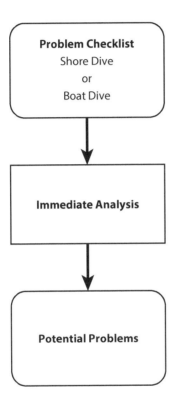

Figure 4.2. Immediate analysis procedure for
potential problem identification

Potential Problem Identification: Shipwreck Dive Example

A completed boat dive potential problem identification checklist is shown at Table 4.3. The identified potential problems are related to the Situation Report from the example dive on HMAS *Swan* used in Chapter 3.

Activity	Potential Problems (what-if)	Problem Yes or No
Loading dive boat	Physical injury	No
	Damage to equipment	No
Boat passage	Man overboard	No
	Rough seas	No
	Fire on board	No
	Sea sickness	No
	Diver injured during boat passage	No
Dressing for the dive	Incorrect assembly of equipment	No
	Incorrect fitting of equipment	No
	Critical equipment missing	No
Water entry from boat	Gas not turned on	No
	Diver injured on water entry	No
	Diver unable to stay on surface	No
	Divers swept away by surface current	No
	Diver forgot equipment	No
Descent to bottom	Descent uncontrolled	No
	Divers separated	No
	Bubble leak from scuba	No
Activity on bottom	Divers separated	**Yes**
	Diver runs out of breathing gas	**Yes**
	Divers attacked by marine life	No
	Diver unwell	No
	Exceeding no-decompression limit	**Yes**
	Silt out inside wreck	**Yes**
	Nitrogen narcosis	**Yes**
Ascent to surface	Ascent uncontrolled	No
	Overhead environment	No
	Decompression sickness	**Yes**
Water exit to boat	Diver surfaces considerable distance from boat	No
	Diver swept away by current	No
	Diver unable to self-exit onto boat	No
Post dive activity	Hypothermia	No
	Diver presenting with decompression symptoms	**Yes**

Table 4.3. Boat dive problem identification checklist

Significant Problem Identification: Shipwreck Dive Example

Deliberate Analysis

Once potential problems have been identified the process continues onto deliberate analysis, which involves analysis of the potential problem in reference to conditions, diver capability and the specific phase of the dive activity. The Situation Report is referred to for this process. The deliberate analysis process may lead to identification of significant problems.

The deliberate analysis process is shown at Figure 4.4.

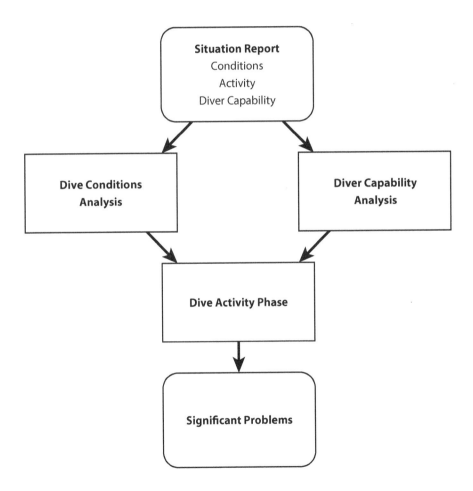

Figure 4.4. Significant problem identification sequence

Significant Problem Benchmarks

For a problem to be considered significant it must be considered probable from all of the perspectives outlined at Table 4.5.

Benchmarks	Descriptor
Occurrence	Probability of occurrence is perceived to exist with the support of situational parameter evidence
Outcome	Probability that it may lead to serious harm or fatality to the diver and/or failure of task
Lack of mitigation	Measures to mitigate the problem are unknown

Table 4.5. Significant problems

Dive Conditions Analysis

From the Situation Report of the shipwreck dive in Chapter 3, key conditions elements are extracted. These key elements will influence the conduct of the dive (the dive activity) and enable potential problems to be identified in advance for further management. The conditions analysis process is shown at Table 4.6.

Key Conditions Elements	Potential Problems	Is it a significant problem? Yes or No
Wreck made safe for recreational divers	Although the shipwreck has been made safe for recreational divers: • The water surface is not directly accessible from the inside of the shipwreck • There is the potential for silt outs inside the wreck • There is the potential for collapsing internal shipwreck structures	Yes
Maximum depth 30 metres	It is a deep dive for recreational divers with associated problems such as nitrogen narcosis, decompression sickness and gas management	Yes
2 x dives planned for the day	Multiple deep dives in one day are potentially problematic from the perspective of decompression sickness	Yes

Table 4.6. Conditions analysis

Diver Capability Analysis

The diver capability analysis follows on from the dive conditions analysis. This is shown at Table 4.7. No significant problems emerge.

Key Diver Capability Elements	Potential Problems	Is it a significant problem? Yes or No
Qualified to Advanced Open Water	No potential problems identified	No
Fit to dive	No potential problems identified	No
Have completed over 100 open water dives	No potential problems identified	No
Have completed dives within last 3 months	No potential problems identified	No

Table 4.7. Diver capability analysis

Dive Activity Analysis

The dive activity analysis uses information from the conditions analysis and diver capability analysis. This information is then applied to analyse the dive activity and determine whether the identified problems are significant. The result of this process is shown at Table 4.8.

Key Activity Elements	Potential Problems	Is it a significant problem? Yes or No
Activity on bottom	Divers separated	Yes
	Diver runs out of breathing gas	Yes
	Exceeding no-decompression limit	Yes
	Silt out inside wreck	Yes
	Nitrogen narcosis	Yes
Ascent to surface	Decompression sickness	Yes
Post dive activity	Diver presenting with decompression symptoms	Yes

Table 4.8. Activity problem analysis

Analysis Conclusion

Analysis of the above tables indicates that the related problems are likely to occur on the dive during activity on the bottom and may continue during the ascent and immediately following the dive.

Decision to Conduct Risk Management

At this point a decision needs to be made in relation to the significance of the identified problem(s). If a problem is perceived as significant, it should be subjected to the next level of risk management.

The significant problem decision process is shown at Figure 4.9.

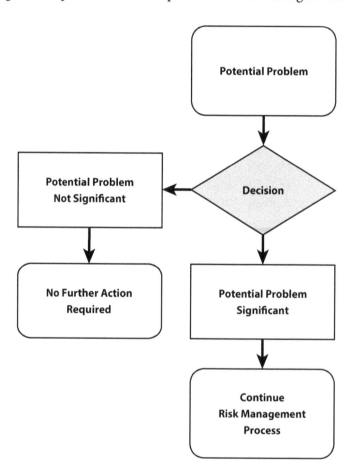

Figure 4.9. Decision process

Checklist templates that can be used to conduct significant problem identification are provided in the Risk Management Toolkit at *page 120*.

Exercise — Identify Dive Related Problems

Construct a dive problem identification checklist for a future dive specific to your interest. Examples you may wish to choose are as follows:
- A future challenging dive of your choice from shore or boat.
- Search and recovery of a lost outboard motor in 10 metres depth.
- A decompression dive to 60 metres.
- A cave penetration dive.

Chapter 5 — Identify and Describe the Risk

At this stage, the significant problem identification requires further breakdown analysis and evaluation. Chapter 5 will explain how to translate the narrative *from a problem to a risk* by identification and definition.

IDENTIFY AND DEFINE THE RISK

Introduction

A significant problem is essentially a situation surrounded by uncertainty which may represent a threat to safety and successful completion of tasks. The first step in the removal of that uncertainty is the translation of the problem into a risk so it can be defined into its key elements.

This chapter explains how a significant problem is translated into a risk for definition. This is a very important step in risk management. Accurate definition of the risk facilitates accurately targeted solutions to the problem. It is also the gateway to other risk related functions such as incident investigation, dive planning, emergency management and much more.

On completion of this chapter, you should be able to define a risk by way of its cause, event and effect.

Risk Identification

Risk

Risk is the combination of cause, event, and effect. Risk is also synonymous to uncertainty which results in a deviation from the expected effect to the unwanted effect, as shown in Figure 5.1.

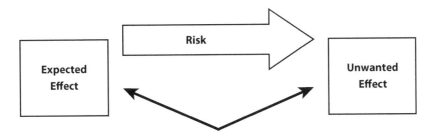

Figure 5.1. Risk deviation from the expected

Risk Elements

A significant problem is translated into a risk by defining the three elements, as follows:

- Cause — why does it happen?
- Event — what may happen?
- Effect — what is the outcome?

The three elements, which make up the risk, evolve from the identified significant problem, as shown at Figure 5.2.

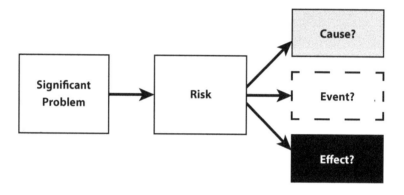

Figure 5.2. Risk and its elements

In relation to scuba diving, risk elements may result from the following situational factors:

- Dive conditions.
- Diver capability.
- Dive activity.
- Individual perception (refer to Risk Perception in Chapter 2).

Risk Chronological Sequence

From a chronological perspective, cause leads to an event which in turn leads to an effect. The chronological sequence is shown at Figure 5.3.

Figure 5.3. Chronological relationship between cause, event and effect

This chronological relationship is important because it enables the understanding of risk mitigation and how it can be used to reduce the probability of an event and the severity of its effect. We will come to more detailed information on cause and effect analysis in Chapter 14, Risk Investigations.

The shipwreck example which follows is used to explain the event, its cause and effect in more detail.

Problem and Risk Elements: Shipwreck Dive Example

In Chapter 4, the conditions, diver capability and activity analysis identified the following significant problems:
- Diver separated.
- Diver runs out of breathing gas.
- Exceeding no-decompression limit.
- Silt out inside wreck.
- Nitrogen narcosis.
- Decompression sickness.
- Diver presenting with decompression sickness symptoms.

Consequently, one key problem that is selected, as an example, for risk identification is "Diver runs out of breathing gas." This is a common problem. In shallow water it is just a simple matter of surfacing. However, when in deep water and inside a shipwreck, the problem is more complicated and can quickly escalate towards a fatality.

Risk

During the "Activity on the bottom," it is anticipated that on a dive to 30 metres, inside a shipwreck, a diver may run out of breathing gas. In relation to the conditions, activity, and diver capability, it is decided that the significant problem is also the event, as shown at Figure 5.4.

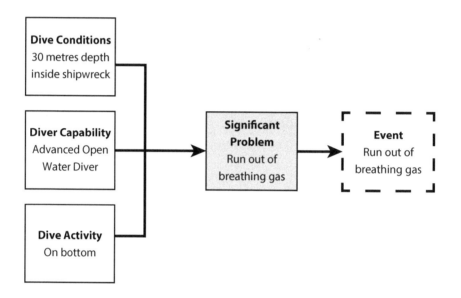

Figure 5.4. Significant problem and risk relationship

Cause of Event

Having established the event, we now determine the cause. There may be a single cause or multiple causes. In the example, if we run out of breathing gas it could be for several reasons, such as: no gas plan; failure to follow the gas plan; gas leak in scuba unit; failure to monitor the contents gauge; faulty contents gauge, etc.

The relationship between the cause and the event is shown at Figure 5.5.

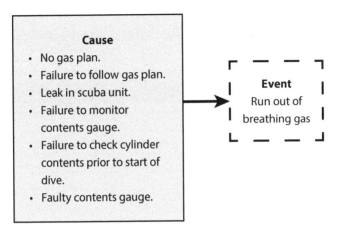

Figure 5.5. Event and cause relationship

Effect of Event

The effect resulting from the event is harm to the diver. For example, diver drowns, etc.

The relationship between event and effect is shown at Figure 5.6

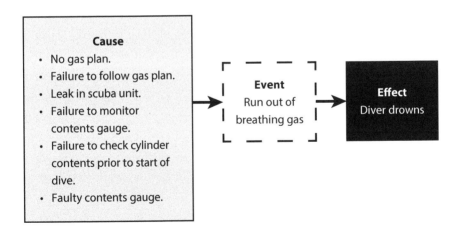

Figure 5.6. Event and effect relationship

Recording Risk Description in the Risk Register

The risk description record is shown at Table 5.7 as it would appear in the Risk Register.

Cause	Event	Effect
No gas plan. Failure to follow gas plan. Leak in scuba unit. Failure to monitor contents gauge. Failure to check cylinder contents prior to start of dive. Faulty contents gauge.	Diver runs out of breathing gas while underwater.	Diver drowns

Table 5.7. Risk identification and description

Exercise — Identify and Describe the Risk

1. With reference to Chapters 3, 4 and 5, and using the shipwreck example, determine the following for the event "Diver experiences nitrogen narcosis":
   a. Cause
   b. Event
   c. Effect

2. With reference to Chapters 3, 4 and 5, and using the shipwreck example, determine the following for the event — "Diver exceeds the no-decompression limit":
   a. Cause
   b. Event
   c. Effect

Chapter 6 — Existing Risk Mitigation

Chapter 6 will explain how *existing risk mitigation* is identified and how it is used to reduce the probability of the event.

IDENTIFY EXISTING RISK MITIGATION

Introduction

An identified and defined significant risk may already have in place mitigation measures. It is therefore important to know what they are and exactly how they mitigate the risk. This chapter explains existing risk mitigation identification and its role in managing risk. In addition, it explains how existing risk mitigation is analysed for adequacy in managing the risk.

On completion of this chapter, you should be able to identify existing risk mitigations that reduce the probability of the event and subsequently the severity of the effect.

Existing Risk Mitigation

Existing risk mitigation are measures that already exist to:
- Reduce the probability of the event occurring.
- Reduce the severity of the effect.

The relationship of risk mitigation during the risk continuum from cause to effect is shown at Figure 6.1.

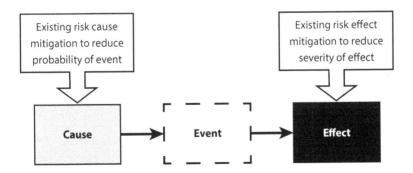

Figure 6.1. Relationship of existing mitigation, cause, event and effect

Risk Mitigation Identification

Some existing risk mitigations that may be identified and which reduce the probability of the event and effect severity of the risk, are shown at Table 6.2.

Activity	Event	Existing Cause Mitigation	Existing Effect Mitigation
Loading/ unloading boat	Physical injury during loading/ unloading boat	Assistance in loading boat	Administer first aid
	Damage to equipment during loading/unloading boat	Assistance in loading boat	Check equipment for damage
Boat passage	Man overboard		Maintain watch for man overboard. Man, overboard procedure.
	Rough seas	Monitor marine weather forecast	Abort dive
	Fire on board	Smoking policy	Emergency procedure for fire incident
	Sea sickness	Motion sickness medication	Administer first aid
	Diver injured during boat passage	Embarkation safety brief	Administer first aid
Dressing for the dive	Incorrect assembly of equipment	Dive buddy check	
	Incorrect fitting of equipment	Dive buddy check	
	Critical equipment missing	Dive buddy check	
Water entry from boat	Gas not turned on	Dive buddy check	
	Diver injured on water entry		Diver water recovery procedure. Administer first aid.
	Diver unable to stay on surface	Use of buoyancy compensator to stay afloat	Standby rescue diver
	Divers swept away by surface current	Predive current check	Diver water recovery procedure
	Diver forgot equipment item	Dive buddy check. Dive Master check.	
Descent to bottom	Descent uncontrolled	Use of buoyancy compensator to control descent	Buddy diver assistance
	Divers separated during descent	Maintain visual distance and close proximity	Separated diver procedure

Activity	Event	Existing Cause Mitigation	Existing Effect Mitigation
Activity on bottom	Divers separated on bottom	Maintain visual distance and close proximity	Separated diver procedure
	Diver runs out of breathing gas	Monitor contents gauge	Gas sharing via buddy's octopus demand valve
	Diver attacked by marine life	Do not dive alone in shark waters	Buddy diver assistance
	Diver unwell	Maintain visual distance and close proximity	Buddy diver assistance. Terminate dive
	Exceeding no-decompression limit	Monitor depth and time	Administer oxygen, monitor diver and buddy, emergency recompression if necessary
	Silt out inside wreck	Employ guideline in low visibility silt conditions	
	Nitrogen narcosis	Buddy divers monitor each other	Buddy diver assistance
	Diver experiencing hypothermia	Monitor water temperature	Terminate dive if too cold
	Sea sickness	Motion sickness medication	Terminate dive
Ascent to surface	Ascent uncontrolled	Use of buoyancy compensator to control ascent	Monitor diver on surface for signs of DCS
	Surfacing considerable distance from boat	Follow dive brief for ascent location	Diver recovery procedure
	Decompression sickness	Monitoring time and depth	Administer first aid
Water exit to boat	Diver swept away by current		Diver recovery procedure
	Diver unable to self-exit water		Diver recovery procedure
Post dive activity	Diver experiencing hypothermia		Administer first aid
	Diver presenting with decompression symptoms		Administer first aid

Table 6.2. Risk mitigation identification table

Adequacy of Existing Risk Mitigation

The adequacy of existing risk mitigation process is carried out using Table 6.3.

Benchmark	Description
Effective	Must mitigate the risk
Practicable	Able to be implemented without creating other significant risks
Cost effective	Effective in relation to its cost

Table 6.3. Existing risk mitigation adequacy table

If any risk mitigation fails to meet one adequacy benchmark, the existing risk mitigation is deemed inadequate.

Existing Risk Mitigation: Shipwreck Dive Example

Identify, Evaluate and Record Existing Risk Mitigation
Reference to the shipwreck dive to 30 metres as outlined in Chapter 3 is used to demonstrate the identification, evaluation and recording of existing risk mitigation. The results are recorded in two separate tables, one for cause mitigation and one for effect mitigation. It is important to keep them separate.

The recording for cause mitigation identification and evaluation of adequacy is shown at Table 6.4.

Cause	Existing Cause Mitigation	Adequacy of Existing Risk Mitigation
No gas plan	Nil mitigation in place	Inadequate
Failure to follow gas plan	Nil mitigation in place	Inadequate
Leak in scuba unit	Nil mitigation in place	Inadequate
Failure to monitor contents gauge during dive	Currently practicing gauge monitoring	Adequate
Failure to check gas content in scuba tank	Currently checking scuba tank contents prior to dive activity	Adequate
Faulty contents gauge	Currently checking function of contents gauge prior to dive activity	Adequate

Table 6.4. Cause mitigation identification and adequacy

The recording of effect mitigation for identification and evaluation of adequacy is shown at Table 6.5 as it would appear in the Risk Register.

Effect	Existing Effect Mitigation	Adequacy of Existing Risk Mitigation
Diver drowns	1. Currently dive in pairs however not always maintaining maximum 5 metre distance between pair 2. Currently employing octopus demand valve 3. Free ascent to surface	1. Inadequate 2. Adequate 3. Inadequate

Table 6.5. Effect mitigation identification and adequacy

It is concluded that some existing risk mitigation is inadequate. This is important to know as existing risk mitigations and their respective adequacies are factored into the next step, which is risk analysis.

Risk Mitigation Decision

The risk mitigation decision process is shown at Table 6.6.

Existing Risk Mitigation Score	Risk Management Action
All existing risk mitigation is adequate	No further action required
One or more risk mitigation measures are not adequate	Risk management proceeds to RM Level 4 (as per Table 2.1. "Deliberate risk management application levels"). Assess the risk.

Table 6.6. Existing risk mitigation decision table

The existing risk mitigation evaluation process is shown at Figure 6.7.

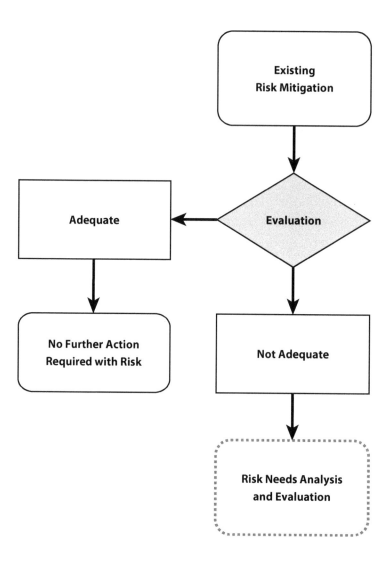

Figure 6.7. Evaluation of existing risk mitigation

Exercise — Determine Existing Risk Mitigation

1. With reference to Chapters 3, 4, 5 and 6, and using the shipwreck example, determine the existing risk mitigation for a diver experiencing nitrogen narcosis.
2. With reference to Chapters 3, 4, 5 and 6, and using the shipwreck example, determine the existing risk mitigation for a diver exceeding the no-decompression limit.

Chapter 7 — Risk Assessment Stage I — Risk Analysis

Chapter 7 will explain the *risk analysis process* in reference to the adequacy of existing risk mitigation.

RISK ASSESSMENT
STAGE I – RISK ANALYSIS

Introduction

Identified risks can be difficult to manage due to individual subjective perception, as discussed in Chapter 2. Perception without a disciplined approach can result in a poor management decision.

This chapter explains a disciplined risk analysis process that enables the risk to be objectively analysed and measured. The process involves the analysis of situational conditions combined with decision tables and metrics.

On completion of this chapter, you should be able to determine the risk level of an identified risk using the risk level analysis table.

Risk Analysis Process

Risk analysis is performed considering risk and existing risk mitigation to determine the risk level.

The risk analysis process is shown at Figure 7.1.

Risk analysis is used to determine the risk level based on two parameters, as follows:

- The probability of the event occurring. Also referred to as risk event probability, event probability, risk probability or probability.
- The severity of the effect emanating from an event. Also referred to as risk effect severity.

The relationship between risk event probability, risk effect severity and risk level is shown at Figure 7.2.

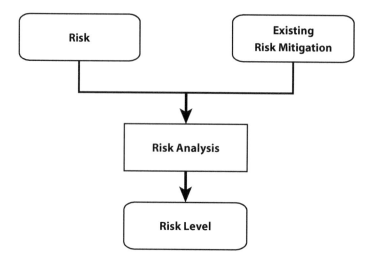

Figure 7.1. The risk analysis process

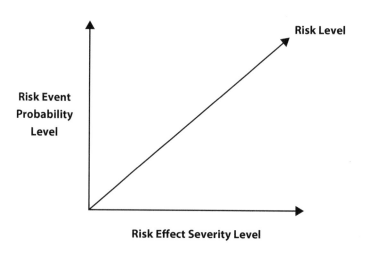

Figure 7.2. Event probability, effect severity, and risk level relationship

Risk Level Analysis Table

The risk level analysis table is a tool used for determining the risk level by cross-referencing risk probability and effect parameters. The risk level analysis table shown at Table 7.3 is specifically designed to cater for dive related conditions and activities. The focus of the table is to determine the level of risk of harm to the diver and/or the failure to complete dive tasks.

The table consists of two scales as follows:

- Risk event probability scale.
- Risk effect severity scale.

Each scale has five levels of magnitude which provides a workable platform for calculating the overall risk level for the identified risk.

	Risk Effect Severity				
Risk Event Probability	Insignificant 1	Minor 2	Moderate 3	Major 4	Catastrophic 5
Highly Probable 5 Greater than 99% but less than 100%	Low 5	Medium 10	High 15	Very High 20	Very High 25
Probable 4 51% to 99%	Low 4	Medium 8	High 12	Very high 16	Very High 20
Possible 3 10% to 50%	Low 3	Low 6	Medium 9	High 12	High 15
Improbable 2 1% to 9%	Very Low 2	Low 4	Low 6	Medium 8	Medium 10
Rare 1 Less than 1% but more than 0%	Very Low 1	Very Low 2	Low 3	Low 4	Low 5

Table 7.3. Risk level analysis

Risk Event Probability Scale

Risk event probability is based on the analysis of situational parameters and the individual's perception of risk.

The probability scale uses a narrative description for each probability level. A percentage scale has also been added to better clarify the narrative descriptor value and is shown at Table 7.4.

Probability	Probability Percentage Descriptor	Probability Narrative Descriptor
Assured	100%	Shall occur in all situations
Highly Probable	More than 99% but less than 100%	Shall occur in most situations
Probable	51% to 99%	Should occur in most situations
Possible	10% to 50%	Should occur in some situations
Improbable	1% to 9%	May occur in some situations
Rare	Less than 1%	May occur in exceptional situations
Impossible	0%	Impossible to occur in all situations

Table 7.4. Risk event probability

In the case of *Assured* and *Impossible* there is no uncertainty about the probability level. *Impossible* is 0%, indicating the risk *cannot* occur and can be ignored. *Assured* is 100%, indicating that the risk *shall occur in all situations*, and naturally needs extra mitigation. *Probable* sits somewhere in-between impossible and assured.

Risk Effect Severity Scale

In relation to a recreational dive, the effects for analysis are considered in two areas, as follows:

- Harm to diver.
- Achievement of task.

Where specific tasks and outcomes are required, achievement of task outcome may be considered. However, it should be noted that harm to diver always takes precedence when considering effect severity during analysis.

The range of the effect scale is shown at Table 7.5.

Effect	Harm to Diver	Achievement of Task
Catastrophic	Death or permanent disability	Task not achieved
Major	Serious injury requiring hospital treatment and considerable lost time (more than a month)	Significant delay to achievement of task
Moderate	Injury requiring hospital treatment and some lost time (less than a month)	Material delay to achievement of task
Minor	Injury requiring medical treatment and minimal loss of time (less than a week)	Inconvenient delay to achievement of task
Insignificant	Injury requiring first aid and no loss of time	Insignificant delay to achievement of task

Table 7.5. Risk effect severity

Risk Level

The risk level is determined using the risk level analysis table by cross referencing the selected probability level with the selected effect level. For example, *Possible* (event probability) and *Moderate* (effect severity) produces a *Medium* risk level.

In addition, a numerical value is allocated to each probability and effect level. By multiplying the number allocated to the respective probability and effect level, a risk level with a numerical score is created. For example:

Rare 1 x *Catastrophic* 5 = risk level *Low* 5.

The risk level numerical score distinguishes the severity of the risk level, for example, a *High 15* denotes a risk level that is relatively more severe than a *High 12*. This provides a more granular score.

The range of risk levels and their respective numerical values are shown at Table 7.6.

Risk Level Narrative	Risk Level Numerical
Very High	16, 20 and 25
High	12 and 15
Medium	8, 9 and 10
Low	3, 4, 5 and 6
Very Low	1 and 2

Table 7.6. Risk level

Risk Analysis: Shipwreck Dive Example

The risk analysis is divided into two stages, as follows:
- Event probability level.
- Effect severity level.

Situation Analysis

The causes of the risk are analysed in the situational conditions of the dive activity, as follows:
- Shipwreck penetration dive.
- Maximum depth 30 metres.
- Advanced Diver qualification with over 100 dives experience.
- Standard recreational dive equipment.

Analysis of the Event Probability Level

The conduct of the analysis of causes is shown at Table 7.7 (with reference to the risk event probability, Table 7.4).

Cause	Existing Cause Mitigation	Risk Probability Level
No gas plan	Nil mitigation in place	Possible
Failure to follow gas plan	Nil mitigation in place	Possible
Leak in scuba unit	Nil mitigation in place	Possible
Failure to monitor contents gauge during dive	Currently practicing gauge monitoring	Rare
Failure to check gas content in scuba tank prior to dive activity	Currently checking scuba tank contents prior to dive activity	Rare
Faulty contents gauge	Currently checking function of contents gauge prior to dive activity	Rare

Table 7.7. Event probability analysis

The decision on the probability level is based on the highest risk probability level recorded. It is therefore decided to select the overall probability level of *Possible*.

Analysis of the Risk Effect Level

The conduct of the analysis of effects is shown at Table 7.8 (with reference to the risk effect severity, Table 7.5).

Effect	Existing Effect Mitigation	Effect Severity Level
Diver drowns	Currently dive in pairs however not always maintaining maximum 5 metre distance between dive pair. Currently using octopus demand valve. Free ascent to surface.	Catastrophic

Table 7.8. Effect severity analysis

The decision on the effect level is based on the highest level recorded which in this case is *Catastrophic*.

Risk Level Calculation

Reference to the Risk Level Analysis Table 7.3, the intersection of the *Possible* row and the *Catastrophic* column provides a calculated risk level of *High 15*.

Recording Risk Level

The risk analysis process is recorded as shown at Table 7.9 as it would appear in the Risk Register.

Event	Event Probability	Effect Severity	Risk Level
Run out of breathing gas	Possible	Catastrophic	High 15

Table 7.9. Risk analysis record

Exercise — Risk Analysis

1. With reference to the shipwreck situation documented at Chapter 3 and using the risk management tools so far discussed, determine risk level for the risk "Diver experiences nitrogen narcosis".
2. With reference to the shipwreck situation documented at Chapter 3 and using the risk management tools so far discussed, determine the risk level for the risk "Diver exceeds no-decompression limit".

Chapter 8 — Risk Assessment Stage II — Risk Evaluation

Chapter 8 will explain how the risk level is *evaluated* to determine if additional risk mitigation is required.

RISK ASSESSMENT
STAGE II – RISK EVALUATION

Introduction

Once a risk has been measured by analysis, it needs to be evaluated against a benchmark to determine if it is acceptable or if it needs further mitigation.

This chapter explains the risk evaluation process using the risk evaluation table. In addition, it discusses the interpretation of the evaluation.

On completion of this chapter, you should be able to determine if a risk is *acceptable* or *not acceptable* and decide on the next course of action.

Risk Evaluation Process

As stated previously, risks are linked to activity. Risks cannot be totally eliminated. There will always be some remaining risk. During a risk evaluation the aim is to determine the threshold at which a risk is accepted or redirected for additional risk mitigation.

In reference to dive activity, the decision to accept a risk is based on the level of risk the diver or the team is willing to accept during the dive activity.

Risk evaluation involves comparing the risk level to the benchmark on the risk evaluation table, as shown at Table 8.1.

Risk Level	Risk Acceptance	Additional Risk Mitigation
Very High	Not acceptable	Required
High	Not acceptable	Required
Medium	May be acceptable	May be required if risk deemed not acceptable
Low	Acceptable	Not generally required
Very Low	Acceptable	Not generally required

Table 8.1. Risk evaluation table

Medium Risk Level

Medium Risk Level Acceptance

Although not generally acceptable, a medium risk level may be accepted in some circumstances. In particular, if the risk level is rated at the lower end of the medium risk level spectrum. This allows the planner some discretion to retain the risk and proceed with the dive activity. Some examples of circumstances are as follows:

- The opportunity presented by the dive activity outweighs the risk of harm to such a degree that it may be justified at a medium risk level.
- The cost of treating the medium risk level is excessive and the risk reduction benefit is minimal.
- Risk perception may play a part in the evaluation of medium risks, for example, a highly experienced dive team may accept a medium level risk.

Situational Awareness for Medium Risk

In circumstances where a medium risk is accepted, divers need to be situationally aware of the elevated remaining risk. Precautions to consider are as follows:

- Confirm divers are qualified, experienced and fit to dive.
- Enhance predive checks.
- Underwater enhanced awareness of risk.
- Confirm emergency procedures are in place.
- Confirm rescue measures are in place.
- Confirm evacuation procedures are in place.

Risk Evaluation Decision

If the risk is deemed acceptable no further action is required and the dive activity may proceed. However, if the risk is deemed unacceptable it will need to be further mitigated. The risk evaluation process is shown at Figure 8.2.

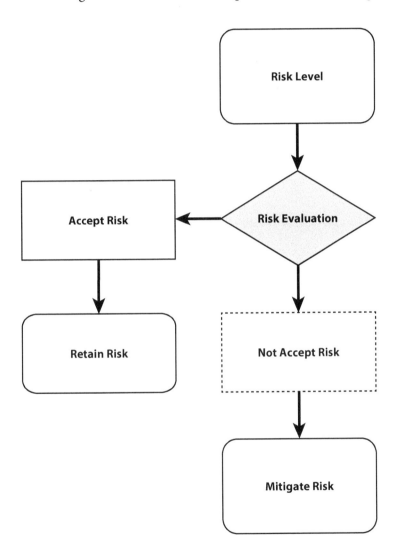

Figure 8.2. Risk evaluation process

Risk Evaluation: Shipwreck Dive Example

From Chapter 6 it was determined that the risk level for the risk "Running out of breathing gas" is a *High 15*. Consequently, reference to the risk evaluation Table 8.1 shows that the risk is not acceptable and will require additional mitigation to lower the risk level to an acceptable level.

Recording the Risk

The risk evaluation is recorded as shown at Table 8.3 as it would appear in the Risk Register.

Event	Probability	Effect	Risk Level	Risk Acceptance	Additional Risk Mitigation
Run out of breathing gas	Possible	Catastrophic	High 15	Not Acceptable	Required

Table 8.3. Risk analysis record

Exercise — Risk Evaluation

1. With reference to the shipwreck situation document described in Chapter 3 and using the risk management tools so far discussed, evaluate the risk level for a diver experiencing nitrogen narcosis.
2. Reference the same shipwreck situation and using the risk management tools so far discussed, evaluate the risk level for a diver exceeding their no-decompression limit.

Chapter 9 — Additional Risk Mitigation

Chapter 9 will explain the *additional risk mitigation* process for risks that are deemed not acceptable.

ADDITIONAL RISK MITIGATION

Introduction

When the evaluation process determines that a risk is unacceptable, additional risk mitigation measures can be explored to see if the risk level can be reduced to a level that is acceptable.

This chapter explains the additional risk mitigation process. This involves the use of analysis techniques that have been explained in previous chapters combined with suitable additional risk mitigation.

On completion of this chapter, you should be able to conduct the additional risk mitigation process.

Additional Risk Mitigation Process

Changes

The process involves the improvement of existing and/or the development of additional or new risk mitigation. It is performed on risks that are evaluated as unacceptable.

In Chapter 8 it was determined that the example risk of "Running out of breathing gas" is not acceptable and will require additional mitigation. The objective is to reduce the risk to an acceptable level.

Stages

Additional risk mitigation involves the following stages:
- Identify the existing mitigation.
- Identify the additional risk mitigation options.
- Analyse the risk with additional risk mitigation options in place to determine the new risk level.
- Evaluate the new risk level to determine acceptability.
- Record the additional risk mitigation process.

Options

The additional risk mitigation options are a combination of one or more measures to reduce the risk level for the dive operation:

- Reduce the probability of the risk event occurring through changes in procedure and/or equipment.
- Reduce the severity of risk effect through emergency procedures, emergency equipment, support personnel and response personnel.
- Obtain dive insurance (to cover loss).
- Cancel the dive.

Mitigation involves development of one of the following measures:

- If mitigation already exists but is inadequate adjust it to make it adequate.
- If mitigation already exists and cannot be adjusted to make it adequate:
    - Keep it and develop additional risk mitigation, or
    - Eliminate it and develop new risk mitigation.

Additional Risk Mitigation: Shipwreck Dive Example

Identify Existing Mitigation

Existing risk mitigation from Chapter 6 is shown at Table 9.1. It relates to the risk of running out of breathing gas.

Potential Cause/Effect	Existing Cause/Effect Mitigation	Adequacy of Existing Mitigation
No gas plan	Nil mitigation in place	Inadequate
Failure to follow gas plan	Nil mitigation in place	Inadequate
Leak in scuba unit	Nil mitigation in place	Inadequate
Diver drowns	Dive in pairs however not always maintaining maximum 5 metre distance between dive pairs	Inadequate

Table 9.1. Cause/effect mitigation

Identify the Additional Risk Mitigation Options

In treating the risk of running out of breathing gas, the following options are identified and listed at Table 9.2.

Potential Cause/Effect	Additional Risk Mitigation Option
No gas plan	Develop gas plan policy and procedures
Failure to follow gas plan	Develop gas plan policy and procedures
Leak in scuba unit	Develop policy and procedure for scuba unit bubble check at start of descent
Diver drowns	Develop policy for maintaining maximum 5 metre visual distance between dive pairs so that buddy diver can assist with octopus demand valve and controlled ascent to surface

Table 9.2. Additional risk mitigation options

Record the Additional Risk Mitigation

The additional risk mitigation is recorded as shown at Table 9.3.

Potential Cause/Effect	Existing Cause Mitigation	Adequacy of Existing Risk Mitigation	Additional Risk Mitigation
No gas plan	Nil mitigation in place	Inadequate	Develop gas plan policy and procedures
Failure to follow gas plan	Nil mitigation in place	Inadequate	Develop gas plan policy and procedures
Leak in scuba unit	Nil mitigation in place	Inadequate	Develop policy and procedure for scuba unit bubble check at start of descent
Diver drowns	Not always maintaining maximum 5 metre distance between dive pairs	Inadequate	Develop policy for maintaining maximum 5 metre visual distance between dive pairs so that buddy diver can assist with octopus demand valve and controlled ascent to surface

Table 9.3. Additional risk mitigation

Assess Additional Risk Mitigation for Adequacy

For an additional risk mitigation to be adequate at reducing the risk level, it must meet the adequacy benchmark shown at Table 9.4.

Benchmark	Descriptor
Effective	Must mitigate the risk
Practicable	Able to be implemented without creating other significant risks
Cost effective	Effective in relation to its cost

Table 9.4. Additional risk mitigation adequacy

The assessment process for additional risk mitigation options is shown at Table 9.5.

Additional Risk Mitigation Options	Effective	Practicable	Cost Effective
Develop gas plan policy and procedures	Yes	Yes	Yes
Develop policy and procedure for scuba unit bubble check at start of descent	Yes	Yes	Yes
Develop policy for maintaining maximum 5 metre visual distance between pairs so that buddy diver can assist with octopus demand valve and controlled ascent to surface	Yes	Yes	Yes

Table 9.5. Additional risk mitigation suitability

Determine Adequacy of Additional Risk Mitigation

Based on the assessment of the additional risk mitigation options, it is determined that they are all adequate for the purpose. This is recorded as shown at Table 9.6.

N.B. The additional risk mitigations identified in this example are specific to the situational analysis outlined in the book. You should develop your own additional mitigations for specific dive situations that may be encountered in the future.

Potential Cause/Effect	Additional Risk Mitigation	Adequacy of Additional Risk Mitigation
No gas plan	Develop gas plan policy and procedures	Adequate
Failure to follow gas plan	Develop gas plan policy and procedures	Adequate
Leak in scuba unit	Develop policy and procedure for scuba unit bubble check at start of descent	Adequate
Diver drowns	Develop policy for maintaining maximum 5 metre visual distance between dive pairs so that buddy diver can assist with octopus demand valve and assist with controlled ascent to surface	Adequate

Table 9.6. Adequacy of additional risk mitigation

Review of Risk Analysis

Having completed the additional risk mitigation, we now conduct a review of the risk analysis, using the table from Chapter 7, to determine if the mitigation has reduced the risk level.

Risk Event Probability	Risk Effect Severity				
	Insignificant 1	Minor 2	Moderate 3	Major 4	Catastrophic 5
Highly Probable 5 Greater than 99% but less than 100%	Low 5	Medium 10	High 15	Very High 20	Very High 25
Probable 4 51% to 99%	Low 4	Medium 8	High 12	Very high 16	Very High 20
Possible 3 10% to 50%	Low 3	Low 6	Medium 9	High 12	High 15
Improbable 2 1% to 9%	Very Low 2	Low 4	Low 6	Medium 8	Medium 10
Rare 1 Less than 1% but more than 0%	Very Low 1	Very Low 2	Low 3	Low 4	Low 5

Table 9.7. Risk level analysis (Table 7.3 from Chapter 7)

Review of Risk Probability Level

The review of the risk probability level following additional risk mitigation of the causes is shown at Table 9.8. It is determined that by having and following a gas plan the probability of the risk "Running out of breathing gas" is reduced from *Possible* to *Improbable* level.

Potential Cause	Additional Risk Mitigation	Risk Probability Level
No gas plan	Develop gas plan policy and procedures	Improbable
Failure to follow gas plan	Develop gas plan policy and procedures	Improbable
Leak in scuba unit	Develop policy and procedure for scuba unit bubble check at start of descent	Improbable

Table 9.8. Review of risk probability level

Review of Risk Severity Level

The review of the risk severity level following additional risk mitigation of the effect is shown at Table 9.9. It is determined that maintaining a maximum 5 metre visual distance between dive pairs will reduce the following effects, should the diver run out of breathing gas:

- Drowning.
- Free ascent related injury.

The additional risk mitigation should ensure the following outcome:

- Buddy diver is in proximity to assist diver in trouble (with no breathing gas) with octopus demand valve, thus avoiding the need for a free ascent or the effect of drowning.
- Buddy diver can assist diver in trouble with a controlled ascent to the surface with octopus demand valve, therefore avoiding free ascent related injury.

The effect resulting from the additional risk mitigation option is that there may be some aspiration of water by one or both divers during the use of the octopus demand valve requiring some first aid following the dive. For example, the administration of oxygen on the surface.

The effect in this circumstance should reduce effect severity from

Catastrophic to *Insignificant* level as shown at Table 9.9.

Effect	Additional Risk Mitigation	Risk Effect Level
Diver drowns	Develop policy for maintaining a maximum of 5 metre visual distance between dive pairs so that buddy diver can assist with octopus demand valve and assist with controlled ascent to surface	Insignificant

Table 9.9. Review of risk effect level

Review of Remaining Risk level

By making reference to Table 9.7, we see that the risk level is reduced to a *Very Low* 2 level. At this point, the risk level is the *remaining risk level* resulting from the additional risk mitigation.

Record Risk Level Review

The risk level analysis review is recorded at Table 9.10 as it would appear in the Risk Register.

Event	Probability	Effect	Remaining Risk Level
Run out of breathing gas	Improbable	Insignificant	Very Low 2

Table 9.10. Risk analysis record

Review of Risk Evaluation

Review of the risk evaluation involves comparing the risk level to the benchmark from the risk evaluation table from Chapter 8, shown at Table 9.11.

Risk Level	Risk Acceptance	Risk Mitigation
Very High	Not acceptable	Required
High	Not acceptable	Required
Medium	May be Acceptable	May be required if not acceptable
Low	Acceptable	Not generally required
Very Low	Acceptable	Not generally required

Table 9.11. Risk evaluation table (Table 8.1 from Chapter 8)

Recording the Risk

The final risk evaluation is recorded as shown at Table 9.12. as it would appear in the Risk Register.

Event	Probability	Effect	Remaining Risk Level	Remaining Risk Acceptance
Run out of breathing gas	Improbable	Insignificant	Very Low 2	Acceptable

Table 9.12. Risk analysis record

Exercise — Additional Risk Mitigation

1. With reference to the shipwreck situation discussed at Chapter 3 and using the risk management tools so far discussed, mitigate the risk level for a diver experiencing nitrogen narcosis.
2. With reference to the same shipwreck situation and using the risk management tools so far discussed, treat the risk level for a diver exceeding their no-decompression limit.

Chapter 10 — Immediate Risk Management

During the execution of a dive, the diver will be exposed to identified remaining risks and may also encounter unidentified risks. The next chapter explains how risk is managed during a dive using *immediate risk management* principles and techniques.

IMMEDIATE RISK MANAGEMENT

Introduction

During a dive, a diver will be exposed to known remaining risks and potential unidentified risks. As unwanted events present themselves, the diver will have limited time to manage these events.

This chapter explains how risk management is continued during the dive using immediate risk management techniques. Immediate risk management capability is the product of personal qualities, training and experience.

On completion of this chapter, you should be able to state the following:

- The factors critical to dive duration.
- The techniques of immediate risk management.
- The techniques for controlling stress.

Time Criticality During Dive

During a dive, time is restricted by the following two major factors:

- Limited duration of gas supply carried by the diver.
- Limited bottom time due to absorption of inert gases such as nitrogen and/or helium which are contributors to decompression sickness.

Any problems that occur underwater must be treated in a time critical manner. This consequently prevents the diver from using the deliberate risk management procedures as outlined in Chapters 2 to 9.

Application of Immediate Risk Management

The application of immediate risk management enables workable risk mitigation to be implemented, even though it is not perfect. This is achieved in

the following three ways:
- Utilising predive planning and past experience.
- Employing situational awareness during the dive.
- Executing quick decisions.

Predive Planning and Past Experience

Situational awareness and immediate decision-making are facilitated by the following factors:
- Deliberate predive risk management and dive planning. This mentally prepares the diver for unexpected events. For example, the problem checklist can prompt the diver for potential problems that although manageable may need to be noted for possible occurrence.
- Utilising past experiences as a reference in immediate decision-making. For example, managing entanglements with lines, deploying octopus demand valve, overcoming disorientation in water column during ascent, reacting correctly to separation from buddy diver, etc.

Situational Awareness During Dive

Situational awareness during a dive utilises the following skills:
- Balanced perception of the underwater environment.
- Comprehension of a developing adverse situation.
- Prediction of potential risks.
- Immediate development and implementation of risk mitigation decisions.

Situational awareness underwater is limited by the following factors:
- Task loading, for example use of complex or additional equipment such as a rebreather, underwater photography, diver propulsion vehicle, etc.
- Physical and mental stress caused by unforeseen events, such as uncharted sea current, sudden appearance of dangerous marine life, etc.

Quick Decisions

Quick decisions require the following skills:

- Ability to read a rapidly developing adverse situation.
- Developing and accepting a workable decision even if it is not the best.

Controlling Stress

Stress can impede immediate risk management. Indicators of stress in the diver and dive team underwater can be felt or observed. Recognition of stress enables the diver to take measures to control it or abort the dive.

Observed in other team members:

- Fight or flight response.
- Surge of energy.
- Loss of control.
- Jumpiness.

Felt by the diver:

- Memory impairment.
- Reduced concentration.
- Difficulty in decision-making.
- Fear, anxiety, or panic.
- Increased breathing rate.

Stress may be controlled as follows:

- Immediately stop any activity or task.
- Slow down breathing rate to normal level.
- Control buoyancy.
- Identify source of stress.
- Focus on controlling source of stress.
- If necessary, abort dive and ascend to surface under control.

Exercise — Immediate Risk Management

This is a practical session which will hopefully become a habit. On a dive, actively exercise situational awareness in the following ways:

- Actively observe the underwater environment.
- Interpret any developing situational parameters.
- Identify potential problems that may occur.
- Develop quick decisions that you may need to take to resolve potential problems.

Chapter 11 — Risk Management and the Dive Plan

Complex dives and dives where additional tasks are conducted require a formal plan. Chapter 11 will introduce you to the formal *dive plan* and show you how risk management is integrated into it.

Chapter 11

RISK MANAGEMENT AND THE DIVE PLAN

Introduction

Complex dives and/or dives that include the execution of additional tasks require careful planning. During the planning phase deliberate risk management is conducted. At the conclusion of the planning phase, the dive plan and risk management will come together.

This chapter explains how risk management and its integration into the dive plan is conducted using the SMEAC system for both planning and delivery of the dive briefing.

On completion of this chapter, you should be able to produce a dive plan underpinned by risk management.

The Dive Plan

The dive plan is a detailed proposal of how a dive is to be organised and executed. It should detail who, when, where, why, what and how in relation to the dive. It should cover the following:

- Dive supervisor.
- Dive team composition.
- Standby diver (where applicable).
- Task.
- Situation (conditions, activity and diver capability).
- Diving equipment.
- Procedures.
- Breathing gases.
- Dive timeline (descent, activity on the bottom and ascent).
- Decompression procedures (where applicable).

- Task execution.
- Dive cancellation procedures.
- Dive abort procedures.
- Dive emergency procedures.
- Dive rescue procedures.
- Dive evacuation procedures.

A single dive plan can be used for several dives where the location, conditions and activity are similar. Where any of these three elements varies, a new dive plan is required.

Dive Plan Template

Development of the dive plan may initially be conducted with reference to existing rules (policies, procedures and/or legislation). However, in circumstances where problems are detected and rules appear ineffective or increase the problem, risk management may be used to deal with these issues. The result may be a risk decision which enables the dive to be conducted in a manner which reduces the risk to a level that is as low as reasonably practicable and acceptable. Conversely, the risk decision may be to avoid the dive. Assuming that the risk decision is to proceed, it can then be integrated into the dive plan.

A document that can be used for planning and briefing is the SMEAC template. In its simplest form it stands for the following:

S — Situation.

M — Mission.

E — Execution.

A — Administration and Logistics.

C — Control and Communications.

This template was originally developed for military application. However, it is generic and can be used for any situation, including diving operations. The template is dual function in the sense that it can be used for designing the plan and it can also be used as a guide for presentation to the diving team.

Documents Supporting the Dive Plan

In formulating the dive plan the following documents are referred to for integration of information:

- Situation Report (Chapter 3).
- Problem Identification Checklist (Chapter 4).
- Risk Register (Chapter 12).
- Procedures.
- Legislation (as applicable).

The Situation Report enables the formulation of the Situation and Mission parts of the dive plan. The Problem Identification Checklist and the Risk Register assist in the formulation of the Execution part, including contingencies. The Administration and Logistics are then selected to support the Execution. The integration process is shown in Figure 11.1.

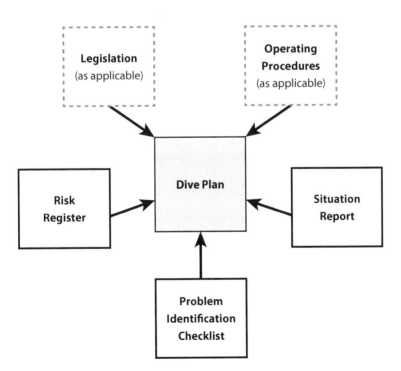

Figure 11.1. Dive plan integration process

Dive Plan Detail

Situation

This is a detailed statement outlining the *conditions*, *activity* and *capability* of the dive team.

Mission

The mission is a brief statement of what is to be *achieved*. It should include the desired *outcome* of the dive.

Execution

This initially consists of a *general outline* of the dive. This is followed by a *detailed explanation*, divided into *phases*, as follows:

- Phase 1 — Preparation
    - General activity.
    - Timings.
    - Contingencies.
- Phase 2 — Move to dive Site
    - General activity.
    - Timings.
    - Contingencies.
- Phase 3 — Descent
    - Dive activity.
    - Timings.
    - Contingencies.
- Phase 3 — Activity on Bottom
    - Dive activity.
    - Timings.
    - Contingencies.
- Phase 4 — Ascent
    - Dive activity.
    - Timings.
    - Contingencies.

- Phase 5 — Move back to shore
    - General activity.
    - Timings.
    - Contingencies.
- Phase 6 — Post dive activity.

The phases of the execution can vary depending on the type of dive and the specific tasks required.

Administration and Logistics

This is an explanation focusing on the following:
- Dive supervisor.
- Dive team composition.
- Standby diver (as required).
- Dive tender (as required).
- Surface support divers (as required).
- Underwater support divers (as required).
- Diving equipment.
- Breathing gases.
- Special equipment (as required).
- Tools (as required).

Control and Communications

This is an explanation emphasising the following:
- Who is in overall control of the dive?
- Who is in control of the dive team underwater?
- How do we communicate from the surface to the divers?
- How do we communicate on the surface?
- How do we communicate underwater?
- Communication plan in an emergency and evacuation.

Integration of Risk Management into Dive Plan

Risk management decisions can be inserted into various areas of the SMEAC template dive plan, as follows:

- Execution.
  - Execution phases — in the form of procedures to reduce the likelihood of risks occurring.
  - Contingencies — in the form of dive cancellation procedures, abort procedures, emergency procedures, rescue procedures and evacuation procedures, to reduce the magnitude of consequences.
- Administration and Logistics.
  - Personnel at dive site — to manage conduct of dive and respond to contingencies.
  - Equipment — to perform the dives safely and to respond to contingencies.
- Control and Communications.
  - Control structure — to manage dives and supervise response to contingencies.
  - Communication system — to facilitate dives and the response to contingencies.

Risk management should enable the optimum development of control measures for risks that are foreseen for the dive.

Attachments to the Dive Plan

Other documents related to diving and attached to the dive plan may be as follows:

- Risk Register.
- Dive gas management plan.
- Decompression plan (where required).

Presentation of Dive Plan

The presentation of the dive plan can be delivered in stages, as follows:
- The Situation and Mission can be delivered separately, well ahead of the dive being conducted, to allow for administration and logistic preparations.
- Administration and Logistics can then also be delivered well ahead of the dive being conducted to allow for preparations.
- The Execution and Control and Communications are delivered just before the dive is to be conducted so that phases and contingencies are fresh in the mind of the dive team. A brief recap of the Mission and update of the Situation can precede the Execution delivery.

Chapter 12 — Risk Management Toolkit

Chapter 12 explains the various *templates* that are available to conduct risk management activities throughout the dive risk management cycle.

.

PART II

PRACTICAL APPLICATION

Chapter 12

RISK MANAGEMENT TOOLKIT

Introduction

Throughout this book risk management principles and techniques have been explained, examples provided and exercises designed to enhance assimilation of knowledge and skill. To employ these principles and techniques in a consistent and meaningful way suitable templates are required.

This chapter introduces then provides the various templates and tables in the "Risk Management Toolkit".

Utilising Software

In practice, risk management will require the recording of a narrative and the creation of various tables. These are most easily created and manipulated using software, for example Microsoft Word and/or Microsoft Excel, but any application which enables you to create, save, and later edit text and tables will be sufficient. In this chapter you will find templates that you can either use as a base, make copies of, or download from the publisher's website.

Download location

All of the following templates are available to download from www.DivedUp.com/diving-risk-management-templates/ (or scan the QR code provided here to open the same page).

Please note: the templates are provided for *download* on an *as-is basis* for *personal and non-commercial use*. While the publisher will happily accept feedback regarding the templates, they are unable to offer any support with using software and no correspondence will be entered into in that regard.

The Toolkit

Situation Report Template

As discussed in Chapter 3.

- The Situation Report Template is on *page 114*.
- A Microsoft Word template file is available to download.

Boat Dive Problem Identification Checklist

As discussed in Chapter 4, this can be used to conduct significant problem identification.

- The template is on *page 116*.
- A Microsoft Word template file is available to download.

Shore Dive Problem Identification Checklist

As discussed in Chapter 4, this can be used to conduct significant problem identification.

- The template is on *page 117*.
- A Microsoft Word template file is available to download.

Dive Plan

As discussed in Chapter 11.

- The template is on *page 118*.
- A Microsoft Word template file is available to download.

Risk Management Decision Benchmark Tables

The risk management decision benchmark tables are used to compare risk judgements made at each risk management level with predetermined and accepted benchmarks.

- The complete range of decision benchmark tables are found starting on *page 120*.
- The Additional Risk Mitigation Suitability Template is found on *page 123*.
- A Microsoft Word template file is available to download.

Risk Register

Tables are the most suitable way to keep a Risk Register. Tables enable risk information to be displayed from initial definition right through to the final risk decision for diving. You might find a spreadsheet a useful way of compiling this information.

Additional columns may be added to the Risk Register to record extra information. The following is a sample of additional column titles:

- Risk Review (which will be covered in chapter 15).
- Person responsible for treating one or more unacceptable risks.
- Date by which risk treatment is to be completed.
- List of supporting documents for each risk (as required), for example, Situation Report, legislation, operating procedures, standards, etc.

An example Risk Register with some risks is shown on *page 124*.
- The Risk Register template is provided on *page 126*.
- Microsoft Excel and Word template files are available to download.

Exercise — Entering Risk Data in the Risk Register

Using the risk data gathered from previous exercises, complete its entry in the Risk Register using the template referenced above.

Exercise — Dive Plan

Using the Situation Report, Risk Register and Dive Plan templates from the Toolkit, produce a dive plan (see Chapter 11) for a significant dive you are considering.

Chapter 13 — Advanced Diving Situational Parameters

Advanced dives introduce *additional situational parameters* that need to be considered in the overall risk management process. Chapter 13 covers a range of situational parameters associated with dive equipment, underwater tasks, deep diving, and rebreathers.

SITUATION REPORT TEMPLATE

See Chapter 3 of *Scuba Diving Operational Risk Management* for an explanation of how and when to use a Situation Report.

Introduction

Background Situation

Mission

Objectives

General Outline

Date/Time Limitations

Type of Dive Activity

Type of Dive Activity	Indicate with Tick
Shore dive	
Boat dive	

Environment of the Activity

Atmosphere		Water		Underwater Terrain - Yes or No	
Air temperature		Temperature		Sand	
Air visibility		Visibility		Mud	
Wind strength		Current strength		Shale	
Wind direction		Current direction		Rock	
		Sea state		Coral	
		Tide level		Seaweed	
		Tidal flow		Caves	
				Walls	
				Slopes	
				Mounts	
				Gutters	
				Chasms	
				Abysses	
				Wreck	

Equipment to be Used

Equipment Category	Specific Equipment Type	Required Yes or No
Thermal protection		
Propulsion		
Life support		
Buoyancy control		
Vision		
Communication		
Time/depth monitoring		
Navigation		
Safety equipment		
Tools		

BOAT DIVE PROBLEM IDENTIFICATION CHECKLIST

Activity	Potential Problems	Problem Yes or No
Loading dive boat	Physical injury	
	Damage to equipment	
Boat passage	Man overboard	
	Rough seas	
	Fire on board	
	Sea sickness	
	Diver injured during boat passage	
Dressing for the dive	Incorrect assembly of equipment	
	Incorrect fitting of equipment	
	Critical equipment missing	
Water entry from boat	Gas not turned on	
	Diver injured on water entry	
	Diver unable to stay on surface	
	Divers swept away by surface current	
	Diver forgot equipment	
Descent to bottom	Descent uncontrolled	
	Divers separated	
	Bubble leak from scuba	
Activity on bottom	Divers separated	
	Diver runs out of breathing gas	
	Divers attacked by marine life	
	Diver unwell	
	Exceeding no-decompression limit	
	Silt out inside wreck	
	Nitrogen narcosis	
Ascent to surface	Ascent uncontrolled	
	Surfacing considerable distance from boat	
	Decompression sickness	
Water exit to boat	Diver surfaces considerable distance from boat	
	Diver swept away by current	
	Diver unable to self-exit onto boat	
Post dive activity	Hypothermia	
	Diver presenting with decompression symptoms	

SHORE DIVE PROBLEM IDENTIFICATION CHECKLIST

Activity	Potential Problems	Problem Yes or No
Dressing for the dive	Incorrect assembly of equipment	
	Incorrect fitting of equipment	
	Critical equipment missing	
Shore water entry	Gas not turned on	
	Diver injured on water entry	
	Diver unable to stay on surface	
	Divers swept away by surface current	
	Diver forgot equipment	
	Difficult entry point to negotiate	
Swim to water descent point	Diver swept away by surface current	
	Divers separated	
	Rough surface conditions	
Descent to bottom	Descent uncontrolled	
	Divers separated	
	Bubble leak from scuba	
Activity on bottom	Divers separated	
	Diver runs out of breathing gas	
	Divers attacked by marine life	
	Diver unwell	
	Exceeding no-decompression limit	
	Silt out inside wreck	
	Nitrogen narcosis	
Ascent to surface	Ascent uncontrolled	
	Surfacing considerable distance from shore	
	Decompression sickness	
Swim Back to shore	Diver swept away by surface current	
	Divers separated	
	Rough surface conditions	
Shore water exit	Difficult exit point to negotiate	
Post dive activity	Hypothermia	
	Diver presenting with decompression symptoms	

See Chapter 4 of *Scuba Diving Operational Risk Management* for details of how and when to use these Problem Identification Checklists.

TOOLKIT

DIVE PLAN TEMPLATE

See Chapter 11 of *Scuba Diving Operational Risk Management* for detail of how and when to use a Dive Plan.

Situation

Mission

Execution (inc Phases)

Administration and Logistics

Component	Explanation
Dive supervisor	
Dive team composition	
Standby diver (as required)	
Dive tender (as required)	
Surface support divers (as required)	
Underwater support divers (as required)	
Diving equipment	
Breathing gases	
Special equipment (as required)	
Tools (as required)	

Control and Communications

Component	Explanation
Who is in overall control of the dive?	
Who is in control underwater?	
How do we communicate on the surface?	
How do we communicate from the surface to the divers?	
How do divers communicate underwater?	
Communication plan in an emergency and evacuation situation.	

Attachments to the Dive Plan

Attach any additional documents related to the dive, for example: Risk Register, Dive gas management plan, Decompression plan (where required).

RISK MANAGEMENT DECISION BENCHMARK TABLES

See Chapters 7 and 8 of *Scuba Diving Operational Risk Management* for detail of how and when to use these Risk Management Decision Benchmark Tables.

The tables have been reproduced together in this Toolkit for quick access and ease of use in the risk management process.

Potential Problems Table

Benchmarks	Descriptor
Occurrence	Possibility of occurrence is perceived to exist based on experience without the support of evidence
Outcome	Possibility that it may lead to serious harm or fatality to the diver and/or failure of task
Lack of control	Measures to control the problem are unknown

Significant Problems Table

Benchmarks	Descriptor
Occurrence	Probability of occurrence is perceived to exist with the support of situational parameter evidence
Outcome	Probability that it may lead to serious harm or fatality to the diver and/or failure of task
Lack of control	Measures to control the problem are unknown

Risk Elements Table

Risk Element	Definition	Descriptor
Cause	Situational parameters and events contributing to risk	Why does it happen?
Event	Occurrence or change in a particular set of circumstances	What may happen?
Effect	The outcome of an event affecting objectives	What is the outcome?

Existing Risk Mitigation Adequacy Table

Benchmark	Descriptor
Effective	Must mitigate the risk
Practicable	Able to be implemented without creating other significant risks
Cost effective	Effective in relation to its cost

Existing Risk Mitigation Decision Table

Existing Risk Mitigation Score	Risk Management Action
All existing risk mitigation is adequate	No further action required
One or more risk mitigation measures are not adequate	Risk management moves to Level 4 (as per Table 2.1. "Deliberate risk management application levels"). Assess the risk.

Risk Level Analysis Table

	Risk Effect Severity				
Risk Event Probability	Insignificant 1	Minor 2	Moderate 3	Major 4	Catastrophic 5
Highly Probable 5 Greater than 99% but less than 100%	Low 5	Medium 10	High 15	Very High 20	Very High 25
Probable 4 51% to 99%	Low 4	Medium 8	High 12	Very high 16	Very High 20
Possible 3 10% to 50%	Low 3	Low 6	Medium 9	High 12	High 15
Improbable 2 1% to 9%	Very Low 2	Low 4	Low 6	Medium 8	Medium 10
Rare 1 Less than 1% but more than 0%	Very Low 1	Very Low 2	Low 3	Low 4	Low 5

Risk Event Probability Table

Probability	Probability Percentage Descriptor	Probability Narrative Descriptor
Assured	100%	Shall occur in all situations
Highly Probable	More than 99% but less than 100%	Shall occur in most situations
Probable	51% to 99%	Should occur in most situations
Possible	10% to 50%	Should occur in some situations
Improbable	1% to 9%	May occur in some situations
Rare	Less than 1%	May occur in exceptional situations
Impossible	0%	Impossible to occur in all situations

Risk Effect Severity Table

Effect	Harm to Diver	Achievement of Task
Catastrophic	Death or permanent disability	Task not achieved
Major	Serious injury requiring hospital treatment and considerable lost time (more than a month)	Significant delay to achievement of task
Moderate	Injury requiring hospital treatment and some lost time (less than a month)	Material delay to achievement of task
Minor	Injury requiring medical treatment and minimal loss of time (less than a week)	Inconvenient delay to achievement of task
Insignificant	Injury requiring first aid and no loss of time	Insignificant delay to achievement of task

Risk Levels Table

Risk Level Narrative	Risk Level Numerical
Very High	16, 20 and 25
High	12 and 15
Medium	8, 9 and 10
Low	3, 4 and 5
Very Low	1 and 2

Risk Evaluation Table

Risk Level	Risk Acceptance	Additional Risk Mitigation
Very High	Not acceptable	Required
High	Not acceptable	Required
Medium	May be Acceptable	May be required if risk deemed not acceptable
Low	Acceptable	Not generally required
Very Low	Acceptable	Not generally required

Additional Risk Mitigation Suitability Template

Additional Risk Mitigation Options	Effective (Yes or No)	Practicable (Yes or No)	Cost Effective (Yes or No)

Additional Risk Mitigation Adequacy Table

Benchmark	Descriptor
Effective	Must treat the risk
Practicable	Able to be implemented without creating other significant risks
Cost effective	Effective in relation to its cost

Additional Risk Mitigation Decision Table

Additional Risk Mitigation Score	Risk Management Action
All existing risk mitigation is adequate	No further action required
One or more risk mitigation measures are not adequate	Consider cancelling the dive

RISK REGISTER EXAMPLE

Situation	Risk			Existing Risk Mitigation	
	Causes	Event	Effect	Mitigation	Adequacy
Dive on shipwreck at 30 metres involving wreck penetration	1. No gas plan. 2. Failure to follow gas plan 3. Leak in scuba unit 4. Failure to monitor contents gauge 5. Failure to check scuba unit gas content prior to start of dive 6. Faulty contents gauge	Diver runs out of breathing gas while underwater	Diver drowns	**Cause Mitigation** 1. Nil mitigation in place 2. Nil mitigation in place 3. Nil mitigation in place 4. Currently practicing gauge monitoring 5. Currently checking scuba tank content prior to dive activity 6. Currently check function of contents gauge prior to dive activity **Effect Mitigation** 1. Currently dive in pairs however not always maintaining maximum 5 metre distance between dive pairs 2. Currently employing octopus demand valve 3. Free ascent to surface	**Cause Mitigation** 1. Inadequate 2. Inadequate 3. Inadequate 4. Adequate 5. Adequate 6. Adequate **Effect Mitigation** 1. Inadequate 2. Adequate 3. Inadequate
Dive on shipwreck at 30 metres involving wreck penetration	1. Faulty dive computer 2. Incorrectly used dive computer 3. Delayed ascent due to concurrent dive incident	Diver exceeds no-decompression limit	Diver experiences decompression sickness following ascent to surface	**Cause Mitigation** 1. Check computer against dive buddy computer 2. As above 3. Nil in place **Effect Mitigation** Emergency decompression stop procedure	**Cause Mitigation** 1. Adequate 2. Adequate 3. Inadequate **Effect Mitigation** Adequate
Dive on shipwreck at 30 metres involving wreck penetration	Diver susceptible to nitrogen narcosis at 30 metres	Diver experiences nitrogen narcosis	1. Diver falls asleep on bottom 2. Diver entangled on shipwreck fixtures 3. Diver drowns	**Cause Mitigation** 1, 2 & 3: Dive pair monitor each other for narcosis during dive **Effect Mitigation** As above	**Cause Mitigation** 1, 2 & 3: Adequate **Effect Mitigation** Adequate

| Risk Assessment | | | | Additional Risk Mitigation | | Risk Re-assessment | | | |
| Risk Analysis | | | Risk Evaluation | | | Risk Analysis | | | Risk Evaluation |
Prob-ability Level	Effect Level	Risk Level	Risk Acceptance	Mitigation	Adequacy	Prob-ability Level	Effect Level	Risk Level	Remaining Risk Acceptance
Possible	Cata-strophic	High 15	Not acceptable	**Cause Mitigation** 1 & 2: Develop gas plan policy and procedure 3: Develop policy and procedure for scuba unit bubble check at start of descent **Effect Mitigation** 1, 2 & 3: Develop policy for main-taining maximum 5 metre visual distance between dive pairs	**Cause Mitigation** 1 & 2: Adequate 3: Adequate **Effect Mitigation** 1, 2 & 3: Adequate	Improb-able	Insignif-icant	Very low 2	Acceptable
Possible	Cata-strophic	High 15	Not acceptable	**Cause Mitigation** 3: Develop policy to commence ascent from bottom two minutes before reaching NDL	**Cause Mitigation** 3: Adequate	Rare	Insignif-icant	Very Low 1	Acceptable
Possible	Insignif-icant	Low 3	Acceptable						

RISK REGISTER TEMPLATE

Location of dive:
Date of dive:

Situation	Risk			Existing Risk Mitigation	
	Causes	Event	Effect	Mitigation	Adequacy

See Chapter 12 of *Scuba Diving Operational Risk Management* for the detail of how and when to use the Risk Register.

| Risk Assessment | | | | Additional Risk Mitigation | | Risk Re-assessment | | | |
| Risk Analysis | | | Risk Evaluation | | | Risk Analysis | | | Risk Evaluation |
Prob-ability Level	Effect Level	Risk Level	Risk Acceptance	Mitigation	Adequacy	Prob-ability Level	Effect Level	Risk Level	Remaining Risk Acceptance

Chapter 13

ADVANCED DIVING SITUATIONAL PARAMETERS

Introduction

Advanced diving introduces situations that may involve extended duration, increased depth, tasks in addition to the dive, and the use of tools and rebreathers. The level of complexity and associated risks increase exponentially. Consequently, risk management becomes even more critical to the safety and good outcome of the dive.

Chapters 1 to 9 explained the process of deliberate risk management based on the three main situational parameters: dive conditions, activity and diver capability. This chapter explains the analysis of additional situational parameters associated with more advanced dives that introduce additional risks.

On completion of this chapter, you should be able to manage risks associated with advanced dives.

Advanced Dives

Advanced dives involve the following advanced diving parameters:
- Dive equipment.
- Tasks.
- Deep diving.
- Rebreathers.

Risk Management Processes

The advanced diving situational parameters can be managed as follows:
- Identify the potential problems.
- Identify the significant problems.

- Identify the risk from the perspective of cause, event, and effect.
- Identify existing risk mitigation.
- Assess the risk level.
- Evaluate the risk for acceptability.
- If the risk in not acceptable apply additional risk mitigation and re-evaluate for acceptance.

Annexes to Chapter 13

The following annexes explain the respective additional situational risk parameters in greater detail:

- Annex I: Dive Equipment.
- Annex II: Underwater Tasks.
- Annex III: Deep Dives.
- Annex IV: Rebreathers.

Exercise — Advanced Diving Situational Parameters

1. Produce a Problem Identification Checklist for a circular search for a lost outboard motor in 30 metres of water with 1 metre visibility on a silt covered bottom.
2. Identify problems that are significant.

Chapter 14 — Risk Investigations

During the conduct of dives near miss events, incidents and failures may occur which should be *investigated to prevent future repetition* which could result in a fatal accident. Chapter 14 will introduce you to the various methodologies for investigations.

Annex I
DIVE EQUIPMENT

Introduction
Some diving equipment is designed to function in limited conditions. For example, there are regulators that work well in shallow water but not in deep water. When planning an advanced dive, it may be suspected that one or more items of equipment are unsuitable. In this circumstance, a deliberate risk management assessment should be conducted prior to diving.

On completion of this annex, you should be able to determine the suitability of equipment for specific dive conditions.

Equipment Categories
Diving equipment can be classified under the following categories:
- Vision.
- Buoyancy control.
- Life support.
- Thermal protection.
- Propulsion.
- Time/depth monitoring.
- Navigation.
- Safety/emergency.
- Tools.
- Communication.

Source of Information
The suitability and limitation parameters of individual items of diving equipment can be found in their respective manufacturer manuals.

Conditions and Activity
The conditions and dive activities will determine the suitability of equipment. Some examples of conditions that may affect suitability:
- Cold water.
- Low light levels.
- Deep water.

ADVANCED PARAMETERS

Examples of dive activities that may affect suitability of dive equipment:

- Deep diving.
- Night diving.
- Cave diving.
- Mixed gas diving.
- Ice diving.

Dive Equipment Analysis Matrix

Divers may at times dive in conditions that are outside the capability of their equipment. Table 13.1 shows a list of potential problems for various categories of equipment used by divers, where capability may be limited in challenging dive conditions such as greater depth, visibility and low water temperature.

Equipment Category	Equipment Sub-Category	Conditions	Potential Problem
Thermal protection	Wet suit	Cold water less than 10 degrees Celsius	Hypothermia
Propulsion	Fins	Currents	Fatigue
Life support	Unbalanced regulator	Deep dive in cold water	Inadequate gas delivery to diver
Buoyancy control	Recreational buoyancy compensator	Deep dive with heavy photographic equipment	Inability to maintain buoyancy
Vision	Mask	Silt out conditions	Unable to see dive instrument information display
Communication	Hand signals	Silt out conditions	Inability to communicate
Time/depth monitoring	Recreational dive computer	Decompression dive	Diver may be locked out of dive computer for 24 hrs if ascent rate and/or mandatory stop not complied with
Navigation	Compass	Low light level	Unable to read compass dial
Safety/emergency	Recreational safety marker buoy	Deep dive to 90 metres	Safety marker buoy line not long enough to reach surface from bottom
Tools	Small knife	Levering task	Blade too short for use as lever

Table 13.1. Equipment suitability limitations

Risk Management Process

The risk management process for diving equipment is shown at Figure 13.2.

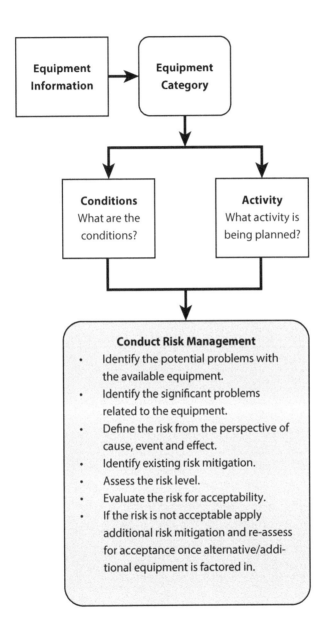

Figure 13.2. Equipment suitability assessment process

Annex II
UNDERWATER TASKS

Introduction

Recreational divers may undertake minor underwater tasks using scuba equipment. These tasks can be considered an additional phase of the dive activity.

On completion of this annex, you should be able to conduct a risk management process in relation to dives that involve underwater tasks.

Potential Tasks

The following is a list of tasks that might be performed during a dive:

- Survey of bottom configuration and composition.
- Searches for lost objects, for example, outboard motor, vessel mooring, anchor, etc.
- Object recovery, for example, outboard motor, lobster pot, anchor, etc.
- Infrastructure inspections, for example small jetties, boat houses, boat ramps, retaining walls, etc.
- Conducting repairs, for example, replacing propellers, anodes, mooring chains, etc.
- Taking photographs or video of marine life, objects, underwater structures, hulls, etc.
- Small vessel hull inspection, cleaning, minor repairs, etc.

Situation

These are the conditions, task and diver's capability to perform the task. The main conditions related to tasks may include one or more of the following:

- Surface water and atmospheric conditions.
- Boat traffic.
- Underwater visibility.
- Depth.
- Currents.
- Bottom composition.
- Dangerous marine life.

For more detail on conditions refer to Chapter 3 — Define the Situation.

Objective

This is the desired outcome at the completion of the task. Expressed in one or more sentences.

Phases

This states who, where, when, what and how the task is to be completed. The task may be actioned in one or more phases, depending on its complexity.

Phase Requirements

To perform the task, certain requirements need to be considered:

- Method for performing the task.
- Duties of each diver.
- Equipment required for performing the task.
- Hazards (problems) relating to performance of task.
- Time allocated to perform the task.
- Location of task.
- Accessibility to task location.

Team Composition

The team composition will consist of the surface component and the underwater component.

The surface components may consist of some of the following:

- Dive supervisor.
- Dive attendant.
- Standby diver.

The underwater component will consist of one of the following:

- Single diver.
- Multiple divers.

Problems Associated with Tasks

In addition to general problems associated with dive activity, when performing tasks additional problems can occur. Some of these are shown at Table 13.3.

ADVANCED PARAMETERS

ADVANCED PARAMETERS

Task	Problems
Survey of bottom configuration and composition	**Underwater** • Diver separation • Spatial disorientation • Silt out on bottom during survey
Underwaters searches for lost objects, e.g. outboard motor, anchor, etc.	**On Surface** • Setting up search equipment and lines **Underwater** • Management of lines • Managing entanglements • Underwater communications • Diver separation • Spatial disorientation • Silt out on bottom during search
Underwater object recovery, e.g. outboard motor, anchor, etc.	**On Surface** • Over-weighting diver with recovery equipment and tools **Underwater** • Entanglement with lifting lines • Entanglement with lift bag during ascent • Run out of gas for lift bag • Object detached from lift bag during ascent • Damage to lift bag • Failure to lift object off bottom • Silt out on bottom during recovery
Infrastructure inspections, e.g. small jetties, boat houses, boat ramps, retaining walls, etc.	**On Surface** • Collision from surface crafts in vicinity of infrastructure **Underwater** • Entanglement with fishing lines • Cuts from sharp components of underwater infrastructure • Confined spaces or overhead ascent barriers of underwater infrastructure

Task	Problems
Conduct underwater repairs, e.g. replace propellers, replace anodes, etc.	**On Surface** • Over-weighting diver with recovery equipment and tools • Tools and/or job parts detach from diver **Underwater** • Buoyancy problems at work site • Drop and lose tools and/or job parts during part fitting phase of task • Zero visibility
Take photographs or video of underwater life, objects, underwater structures, hulls, etc.	**On Surface** • Damage to photographic equipment during water entry and exit • Over-weighting diver with photographic equipment **Underwater** • Buoyancy problems with photographic equipment • Ambient lighting inadequate for photography • Damage of photographic equipment by collision with underwater structures/objects, etc.
Small vessel underwater hull inspection, cleaning, minor repairs, etc.	**On Surface** • Collision from other surface crafts in vicinity • Operating propeller injury • Injury from hot water flowing from hull surface outlets **Underwater** • Injury from operating propeller • Injury from underwater hull protrusions • Entanglement with underwater lines attached to hull • Injury from hot water flowing from hull underwater outlets

Table 13.3. Problems associated with task execution

The risk management process for tasks is shown at Figure 13.4.

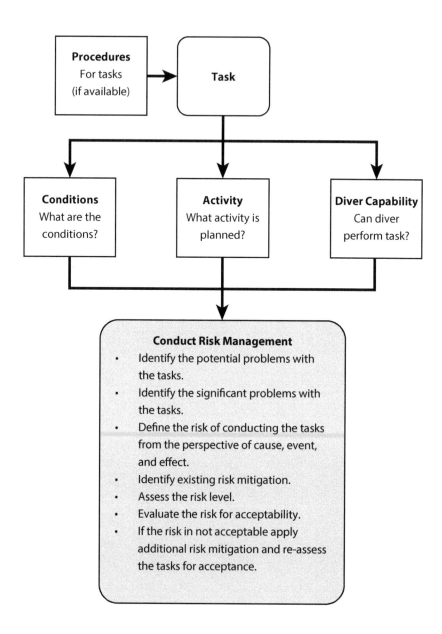

Figure 13.4. Task risk management process

Annex III
DEEP DIVES

Introduction

Diving deeper introduces additional risk for divers. Among many risks are gas endurance of breathing apparatus, exposure to nitrogen narcosis, the potential for decompression sickness and hypothermia to name a few.

At some stage divers will consider diving deeper. This is fine provided that potential problems associated with a deep dive are considered in advance and adequately managed.

On completion of this annex, you should be able to identify and manage risks associated with a dive that is deep in relation to your qualification, experience, equipment and dive conditions.

Qualification and Experience for Recreational Divers

A deep dive is relative to the qualification and experience level of the individual diver. The relationship between qualification, experience and the deep dive limit for recreational scuba diving are shown at Table 13.5. The *Course Experience* column shows the bare minimum requirement. In reality the average person would benefit greatly from completing about 20 additional dives at Open Water level before attempting the Advanced Open Water course and an additional 20 dives before attempting the Deep Diver course. Some individuals may require more than 20 dives at each level.

The examples at Table 13.5 and 13.6 are based on parameters established by recreational diving training agencies. They may vary over time and in different training agencies.

Qualification	Course Experience	Additional Experience	Depth Limit
Open Water Diver	4 dives	20 dives	18 metres
Advanced Open Water Diver	4 dives	20 dives	30 metres
Deep Diver	3 dives		40 metres

Table 13.5. Example recreational diver qualifications, experience and depth limits

Deep Dive Depths

Recreational Maximum Depths
For each qualification, the maximum depth that would be identified as a deep dive and its associated problems are shown at Table 13.6.

Technical Maximum Depths
Dives deeper than 40 metres are referred to as *technical* dives and introduce additional problems as shown in Table 13.7. These examples are based on parameters established by recreational diver training agencies that provide technical courses. They may vary over time and in different agencies.

Deeper Maximum Depths (beyond 100 metres)
Diving deeper than 100 metres is essentially experimental and introduces the following additional problems.
- Increased density of breathing gas.
- Gas management and endurance.
- Free ascent to surface not possible due to decompression obligation.
- Acute oxygen poisoning potential during long decompression stops on high oxygen percentages.
- Increased unreliability of decompression data below 60 metres.
- Higher probability of decompression sickness.
- Hypothermia during very long decompression stops.
- High pressure nervous syndrome on descent below 150 metres.
- On open circuit scuba, isobaric counter diffusion following gas switch to higher nitrogen content gas mix during ascent, potentially inducing decompression sickness.

Qualification	Maximum Depth	Potential Problems
Open Water Diver	18 metres	• No-decompression bottom time is limited beyond 10 metres • Free ascent to surface may be problematic for some divers
Advanced Open Water Diver	30 metres	• No-decompression bottom time is very limited beyond 18 metres • Nitrogen narcosis is problematic to some individuals at 30 metres • Free ascent to surface problematic for most persons
Deep Diver	40 metres	• No-decompression bottom time is extremely limited beyond 30 metres • Nitrogen narcosis is problematic to some persons at and beyond 30 metres • Free ascent to surface is very problematic for most divers

Table 13.6. Maximum depth and associated problems

Qualifications	Maximum Depth	Potential Problems
Advanced Nitrox and Decompression Procedures	45 metres	• Gas management and endurance • Nitrogen narcosis is very problematic to some persons beyond 40 metres • Free ascent to surface is not possible due to decompression obligation • Acute oxygen poisoning potential during decompression on 100% oxygen
Trimix	60 metres	• Gas management and endurance • Free ascent to surface is not possible due to decompression obligation • Acute oxygen poisoning potential during decompression on 100% oxygen
Advanced Trimix	100 metres	• Gas management and endurance • Free ascent to surface not possible due to decompression obligation • Acute oxygen poisoning potential during long decompression times on 100% oxygen • Higher probability of decompression sickness • Hypothermia during long decompression duration

Table 13.7. Deeper dive zones and problems

The risk management process for a deep dive is shown at Figure 13.8.

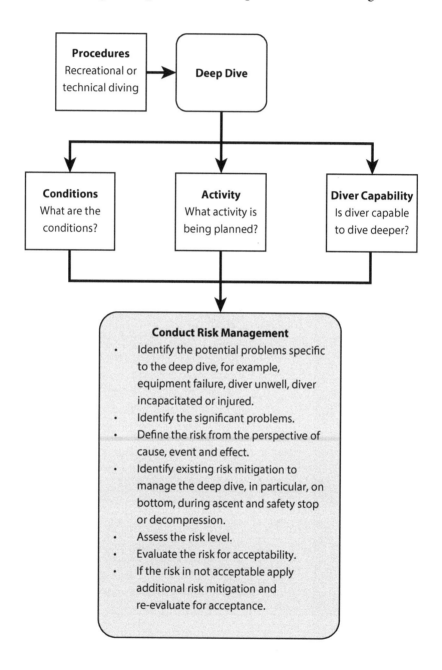

Figure 13.8. Deep dive risk management process

Annex IV
REBREATHERS

Introduction

Rebreathers entered recreational and technical diving around 1995. Prior to that date they were mainly used for military and commercial diving applications. This chapter will outline the three major categories of rebreathers and their associated problems.

On completion of this annex, you should be able to state the operational capabilities of various rebreathers.

Rebreathers and Component Terminology

Nearly 150 years of rebreather use (since 1878) has resulted in their components being identified by various terms. The terms used in this chapter are commensurate with those currently used by recreational and technical rebreather divers. Comparable terms are provided at Table 13.9 for those who may be more familiar with them.

Terms Used Here	Comparable Terms
Open circuit	Aqualung
Closed circuit oxygen rebreather	CCR (oxygen)
Semi-closed circuit mixed gas rebreather	SCCR (mixed gas)
Closed circuit electronic controlled mixed gas rebreather	CCR
Counterlung	Breathing bag
Scrubber	Scrubber canister Carbon-dioxide absorbent canister Soda lime canister Stack
CO_2 absorbent	Carbon-dioxide absorbent Sorb Soda lime
Loop	Breathing loop Breathing circuit
Nitrox	Enriched air
Duration	Endurance

Table 13.9. Comparable terms related to rebreathers

Types of Rebreathers

Rebreathers are a kind of underwater breathing apparatus that recirculates exhaled gas by removing carbon dioxide and adding fresh oxygen prior to inhalation by the diver. Rebreathers are broadly classified into the following general categories based on their operation and type of breathing gas.

- Closed circuit oxygen rebreather — dates from 1878. Used by some recreational divers for long duration shallow diving in special applications.
- Semi-closed circuit mixed gas rebreather — dates from the early 20th century. Wide use by recreational divers starts about 1995.
- Closed circuit electronic controlled mixed gas rebreather — dates from the late 1950s. Wide use by recreational and technical divers starts about 1995.

The characteristics of the various rebreather categories are shown at Table 13.10.

Rebreather Type	General Breathing Gas	General Depth Application	General Duration
Closed circuit oxygen	Oxygen	0–15 metres	1–4 hrs
Semi-closed circuit mixed gas	Nitrox	0–50 metres	1–2 hrs
Closed circuit electronic controlled mixed gas	Nitrox Trimix	0–40 metres 0–150 metres	2–3 hrs

Table 13.10. Rebreather characteristics

Open Circuit

A simplified schematic of an open circuit set is shown at Figure 13.11 as a baseline to compare the complexity of its major components with rebreathers. The major components are as follows:

1. Gas cylinder.
2. Pressure reducing valve (first stage).
3. Demand valve (second stage).

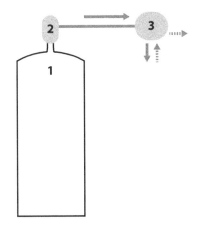

Figure 13.11. Open circuit

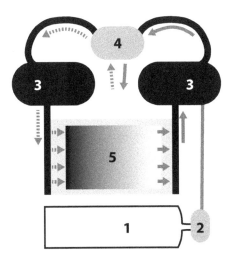

Figure 13.12. Closed circuit oxygen rebreather

ADVANCED PARAMETERS

Closed Circuit Oxygen Rebreather

The oldest of the rebreather designs. Used by some recreational divers in special applications in shallow water.

The closed circuit rebreather for shallow water diving using 100% oxygen (constant flow) is shown in a simplified schematic at Figure 13.12. The major components are as follows:

1. Oxygen cylinder.
2. Pressure reducing valve, constant flow valve, manual gas addition valve.
3. Counterlung.
4. Mouthpiece (with dive/surface valve).
5. Scrubber.

Semi-Closed Circuit Mixed Gas Rebreather

Semi-closed circuit rebreathers were introduced to the general recreational diving community from 1995, however they fell out of favour within a few years. This generally resulted in their use being discontinued in favour of recreational depth closed circuit electronic mixed gas rebreathers. Some manufacturers have introduced newer models aimed at the sport (rather than technical) market in recent years.

The semi-closed circuit rebreather is generally used with nitrox. A simplified schematic of the constant flow model is shown at Figure 13.13. The major components are as follows:

1. Nitrox cylinder.
2. Pressure reducing valve, constant flow valve, manual gas addition valve.
3. Counterlung.
4. Counterlung pressure relief valve.
5. Mouthpiece (with dive/surface valve).
6. Scrubber.

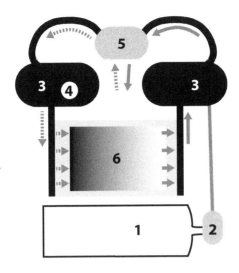

Figure 13.13. Semi-closed circuit mixed gas rebreather

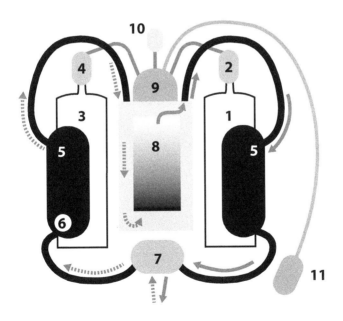

Figure 13.14. Closed circuit electronically
controlled mixed gas rebreather

ADVANCED PARAMETERS

Closed Circuit Electronically Controlled Mixed Gas Rebreather

Introduced to the general diving community from 1995. Currently the most widely used rebreather for recreational and technical diving.

Closed circuit electronically controlled mixed gas rebreathers are available in two general variants:

- Manual control (diver uses a manual gas addition valve).
- Automatic control (computer controls gas addition with a solenoid actuated valve).

A simplified schematic of the version with automatic control is shown at Figure 13.14. The major components are as follows:

1. Diluent gas cylinder.
2. Diluent pressure reducing valve, demand valve, manual gas addition valve.
3. Oxygen cylinder.
4. Oxygen pressure reducing valve, manual gas addition valve.
5. Counterlung.
6. Counterlung pressure release valve.
7. Mouthpiece (with dive/surface valve).
8. Scrubber.
9. Electronic control unit, oxygen sensors, solenoid valve.
10. Oxygen partial pressure meter.
11. Computer.

Comparative Operational Characteristics of Rebreathers

Each category of rebreather has characteristics which make it suitable in specific dive applications. A comparison of rebreather and open circuit scuba characteristics is shown at Table 13.15.

Operational Characteristics	Open Circuit	Closed Circuit Oxygen Rebreather	Semi-Closed Circuit Mixed Gas Rebreather	Closed Circuit Electronic Controlled Mixed Gas Rebreather
Operation	• Demand	• Constant flow • Demand	• Constant flow • Demand	• Constant flow/ manual gas addition • Electronic control/solenoid gas addition
Breathing gases	• Air • Oxygen • Nitrox • Trimix • Heliox	• Oxygen	• Nitrox • Heliox	• Air/oxygen • Trimix/oxygen • Heliox/oxygen
Portability	Cylinders bulky and heavy	Compact and light	Relatively compact and light compared to other systems	Depends on brand and model. Can be relatively compact and light, or bulky and heavy.
Gas endurance	Limited by increasing depth requiring multiple cylinders for long duration dives	Long gas endurance independent of depth	Long gas endurance independent of depth	Very long gas endurance independent of depth
Operational cost of gas	Economical with air or nitrox. Expensive when helium mixes are used.	Economical	About one quarter the cost of open circuit scuba	About one tenth the cost of open circuit scuba
Pre-dive preparation	Simple	Complex	Complex	Very complex
Pre-dive checks	Minimal	Extensive	Extensive	Very extensive
Dive operation	Undemanding	Demanding	Demanding	Very demanding

ADVANCED PARAMETERS

Operational Characteristics	Open Circuit	Closed Circuit Oxygen Rebreather	Semi-Closed Circuit Mixed Gas Rebreather	Closed Circuit Electronic Controlled Mixed Gas Rebreather
Post dive servicing	Simple	Complex	Complex	Very complex
Scheduled maintenance	Uncomplicated	Complicated	Complicated	Very Complicated
Preferred applications	Recreational diving down to 40 metres	Shallow water long duration special application dives	Long duration dives down to 50 metres on nitrox	Deep diving using helium gas mixes down to 150 metres
Weaknesses	Limited gas endurance at greater depths	Restricted time/depth due to acute oxygen toxicity risk	Hypoxia risk if gas flow is restricted or interrupted	• Electrochemical oxygen sensor unreliable • Solenoid addition valve malfunction
Performance Reliability	Very reliable	Reliable	Reliable	Unreliable due to oxygen sensor sudden unexpected failure, requiring open circuit scuba bailout system

Table 13.15. Comparative operational characteristics of rebreathers

Rebreather Dive Activity and Associated Problems

The following tables show the potential problems and underlying causes for the various rebreather groups. These can be used as a source for significant risk identification. Some rebreather designs in certain categories may be more susceptible to particular problems.

Closed Circuit Oxygen Rebreathers

Potential problems associated with closed circuit oxygen rebreathers (constant flow) are shown at Table 13.16.

Activity	Potential Problem	Possible Cause
Water entry	Flooded rebreather loop	• Incorrect assembly of rebreather prior to dive • Physical damage to rebreather components
Descent	Not enough gas in counterlung	• Too rapid descent causing counterlung to compress, reducing volume of breathing gas
Activity on bottom	Inert gas hypoxia	• Failure to flush out air from counterlung prior to entering water • Exhaled nitrogen accumulation in counterlung during dive
	Hypoxia	• Constant flow of oxygen into counterlung restricted or blocked • Oxygen cylinder valve not turned on • Oxygen cylinder empty
	Hyperoxia	• Exceeding safe depth/time limit for breathing oxygen underwater
	Hypercapnia	• Exceeding duration limit of CO_2 absorbent • No CO_2 absorbent in scrubber • Scrubber incorrectly packed
Ascent	Ascent hypoxia	• Failure to flush out accumulated exhaled nitrogen from counterlung prior to ascent
Water exit	Flooded rebreather loop	• Incorrect use of mouthpiece dive/surface valve on surfacing

Table 13.16. Potential problems — closed circuit oxygen rebreather (constant flow)

Globally, there are many different types of closed circuit oxygen rebreathers. Reference to the respective user manuals will indicate where the potential problems are likely to occur throughout a dive activity.

Semi-Closed Circuit Mixed Gas Rebreather

Potential problems associated with semi-closed circuit mixed gas rebreathers (constant flow) are shown at Table 13.17.

Activity	Potential Problems	Possible Cause
Water entry	Flooded rebreather loop	• Incorrect assembly of rebreather prior to dive • Physical damage to rebreather components
Descent	Not enough gas in counterlung	• Too rapid descent causing counterlung to compress, reducing volume of breathing gas
Activity on bottom	Inert gas hypoxia (problematic with mixed gas low flow rate)	• Failure to flush out air from counterlung to entering water • Exhaled nitrogen accumulation in counterlung during dive
	Hypoxia	• Constant flow of mixed gas into counterlung restricted or blocked • Mixed gas cylinder valve not turned on • Mixed gas cylinder empty • Incorrect constant gas flow setting for the selected gas mixture
	Hyperoxia	• Exceeding safe depth/time limit for oxygen percentage in mixed gas underwater
	Hypercapnia	• Exceeding duration limit for CO_2 absorbent • Exceeding depth rating of scrubber • No CO_2 absorbent in scrubber • Scrubber incorrectly packed
Ascent	Ascent hypoxia (problematic with mixed gas low flow rate)	• Failure to flush out accumulated exhaled nitrogen from counterlung prior to ascent
Water exit	Flooded rebreather loop	• Incorrect use of mouthpiece dive/surface valve on surfacing

Table 13.17. Potential problems — semi-closed
circuit mixed gas rebreather (constant flow)

Globally, there are many different types of semi-closed circuit mixed gas rebreathers. Reference to their respective user manuals will indicate where the potential problems are likely to occur throughout a dive activity.

Closed Circuit Electronically Controlled Mixed Gas Rebreather

Closed circuit electronically controlled mixed gas rebreathers rely on electro/chemical sensors and, in some models, a computer to control the delivery of gas to the diver. Potential problems associated with this set-up are shown at Table 13.18.

Activity	Potential Problems	Possible Cause
Water entry	Flooded rebreather loop	• Incorrect assembly of rebreather prior to dive • Physical damage to rebreather components
Descent	Not enough gas in counterlung	• Too rapid descent causing counterlung to compress, reducing volume of breathing gas • O_2 sensor malfunction • O_2 solenoid valve malfunction • O_2 and/or diluent cylinder valve not turned on
Activity on bottom	Hypoxia	• O_2 sensor malfunction • O_2 solenoid valve malfunction • O_2 cylinder and/or diluent cylinder valve not turned on • O_2 cylinder and/or diluent cylinder empty
	Hyperoxia	• O_2 sensor malfunction • O_2 solenoid valve malfunction
	Hypercapnia	• Exceeding duration limit for CO_2 absorbent • No CO_2 absorbent in CO_2 scrubber • CO_2 absorbent canister incorrectly packed • CO_2 sensor malfunction • Exceeding depth rating of scrubber CO_2 absorption capacity when diving very deep
Ascent	Ascent hypoxia	• Solenoid valve malfunction
Water exit	Flooded rebreather loop	• Incorrect use of mouthpiece dive/surface valve on surfacing

Table 13.18. Potential problems — closed circuit mixed gas electronically controlled rebreather with computer control

Globally, there are many different types of closed circuit electronic rebreathers. Reference to their respective user manuals will indicate where the potential problems are likely to occur throughout a dive activity.

Attempts to Make Rebreathers Safer

Since 1995 various manufacturers have attempted to make rebreathers safer and easier to use by the development of the following technologies:

- **Carbon dioxide sensors** to indicate precise duration of carbon dioxide absorbent.
- Addition of **helium sensors** to diversify dependence on oxygen sensors, which are prone to sudden failure.
- Addition of **secondary electronic circuitry** in case of primary electronic circuit failure.
- Addition of **secondary solenoid valves** in case of primary solenoid valve failure.
- Introduction of the more reliable **electro optical oxygen sensor** to replace the electro chemical oxygen sensors which are prone to sudden failure.
- **Hybrid gas delivery systems** combining manual valve gas addition with computer control solenoid valve gas addition.
- **Automatic predive system check** and oxygen sensor check.

While this has improved safety in some situations, rebreathers remain complex apparatus with numerous potential failure points.

Rebreather Risk Management

Analysis of rebreather limitations, dive conditions, dive activity and diver capability should enable the diver to identify significant problems that may occur during the dive. These identified problems can then be translated into risk narrative for risk management. The process for risk management of a rebreather is shown at Figure 13.19.

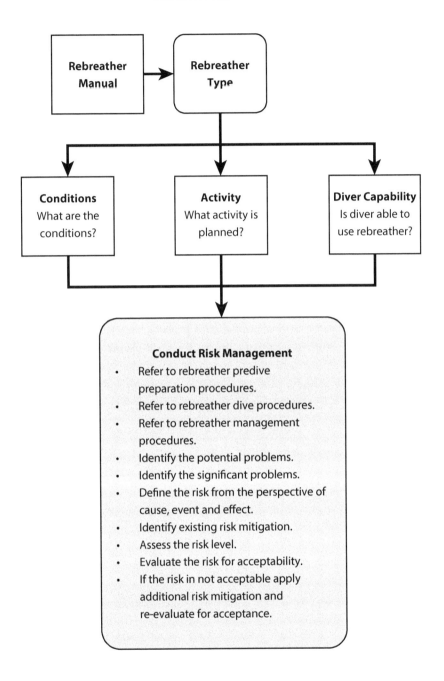

Figure 13.19. Rebreather risk management process

Chapter 14

RISK INVESTIGATIONS

Introduction

During a dive a near miss or incident may occur which needs to be investigated to better manage the risk in the future.

This chapter introduces risk investigation techniques that have evolved from the failure mode, effects and criticality analysis (FMECA) methodology that was originally developed for preventing undesirable events. The risk investigation methods have subsequently been developed for investigating the *occurrence* of the event to determine the *root cause* and the potential *effect*.

On completion of this chapter, you should be able to conduct reviews and investigations related to diving procedures, failures and incidents. In this context, an incident is an event that has unintentionally occurred, but has not resulted in serious damage, serious injury or loss of life.

Aims

The aim of the risk investigation is to determine the cause and effect of the event. This enables the development of mitigation measures for future dive management.

Risk investigations may be in the following areas:

- Dive procedure review.
- Post dive incident investigation.
- Task failure investigation.
- Dive equipment failure.

Trigger for Investigation

The trigger for conducting an investigation may be one or more of the following effects:

- Complaint from diver(s).
- Dive incident.
- Failure of task.
- Equipment failure.

The trigger will provide the following known elements that create the risk:
- Event.
- Operational effect.

The unknown elements which are the subject of investigation are the cause(s) and potential strategic effects, as shown in Figure 14.1.

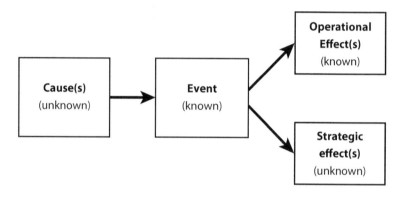

Figure 14.1. Known and unknown elements

Analysis Tools

Risk investigations involve the use of quality management tools that have been further developed by various manufacturing industries following the original development of FMECA. These tools are very adaptable to dive investigations. They are as follows:
- Cause analysis tools.
- Event and effect analysis tools.

They are acknowledged and described in the *IEC/ISO 31010 International Standard Risk management — Risk assessment techniques* (Edition 1, 2009–11).

Cause Analysis

Cause analysis involves the use of quality management tools to identify the number of cause categories and the root cause of the risk event. Two useful tools are:

- Cause category mapping.
- Root cause analysis.

Cause Category Mapping

Cause category mapping is a method that utilises a cause and effect diagram to facilitate the identification of cause categories and their respective cause sub-categories, as shown at Figure 14.2.

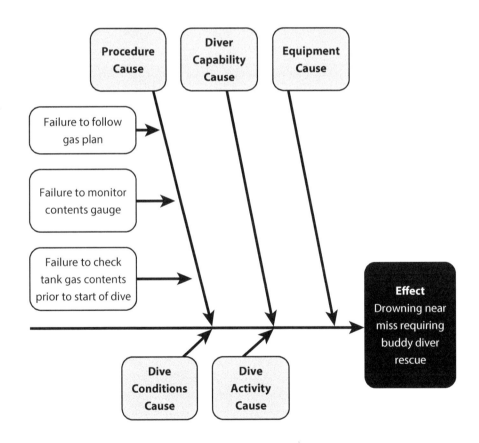

Figure 14.2. Cause category mapping

Root Cause Analysis

Within each cause category, sub-categories can be investigated through a process known as root cause analysis. This process asks the question "Why?" in a repeated sequence until the root cause of the risk event is identified.

An example of the root cause analysis process is shown at Figure 14.3 for a leak in a scuba unit.

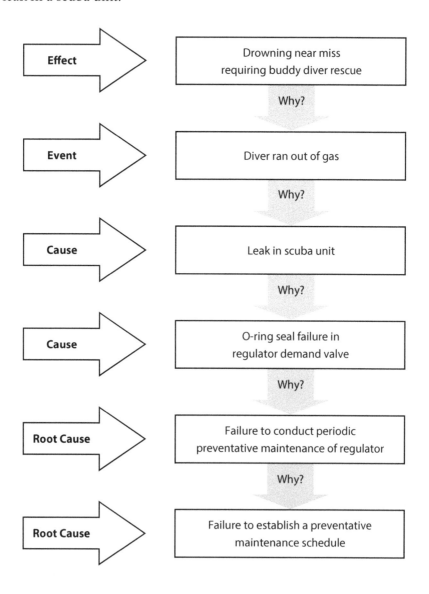

Figure 14.3. Root cause analysis

Development of Risk Mitigation

Analysis of each cause factor enables the development of risk mitigation as shown at Table 14.4.

Cause Factor	Risk Mitigation
Leak in scuba unit	• Conduct predive check of scuba unit for serviceability • Conduct bubble check in water prior to descent to bottom
O-ring seal failure	• Schedule periodic preventative maintenance of regulator and scuba tank
Failure to conduct periodic preventative maintenance of regulator	• Establish log of regulator and scuba unit maintenance

Table 14.4. Risk mitigation

Event and Effect Analysis

This technique is used to identify potential strategic complications which may occur if the problem/risk is not resolved. A future repetition of the event may result in drowning or serious injury during rescue, for example a burst lung. This has strategic consequences which may continue for hours, days, weeks, months or years following the event, as shown at Figure 14.5.

INVESTIGATIONS

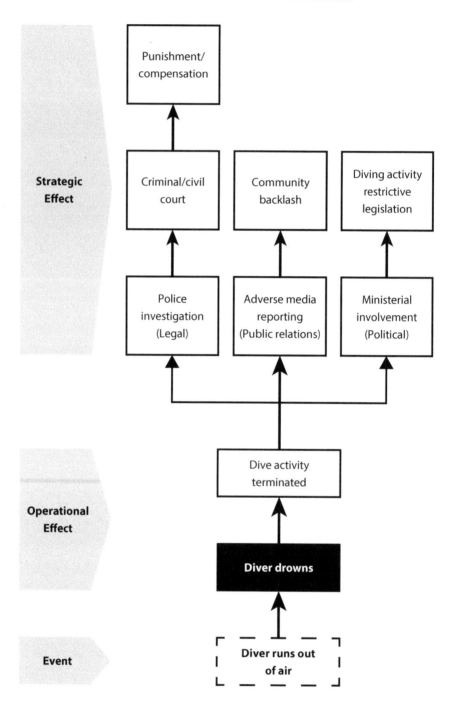

Figure 14.5. Subsequent effect analysis mapping

Other potential strategic effect categories are as follows:

- Medical — relates to the ongoing medical treatment of the seriously injured diver.
- Lifestyle — relates to the ongoing impact on the lifestyle of the seriously injured diver.
- Organisational — relates to the ongoing impact on the diving group's continuing existence.
- Economic — relates to the cost of the ongoing effect for the individual and/or group.
- Reputational — relates to the impact on the individual's and/or the group's reputation.

Annexes to Chapter 14

The following annexes outline the processes involved in specific investigations in greater detail:

- Annex I: Dive Procedures Review.
- Annex II: Post Dive Incident or Near Miss.
- Annex III: Task Failure.
- Annex IV: Dive Equipment Failure.

Exercise — Risk Investigation

Investigate a near miss event, a failed task or an incident which occurred on a previous dive.

Chapter 15 — Risk Monitor and Review

During a period of dive activity situational parameters can change. Consequently, dive activities need to be continuously *monitored* so that changes can be detected, and risk mitigation modified in situ. In addition to monitoring, regular *debriefs* should be used to *review* completed activity and determine if risk mitigation is still valid. Chapter 15 explains the process of risk monitoring and review.

Annex I
DIVE PROCEDURES REVIEW

Introduction

A dive group may have written standard operating procedures (SOPs). Over time a SOP may become outdated as new techniques and technology are introduced into the diving community. Also, the SOPs may not work in all circumstances and therefore require temporary modification.

On completion of this annex, you should be able to conduct a dive procedure review.

Standard Operating Procedures

The following is a list of sub-categories that may be covered in a dive SOPs document:

- Dive responsibilities.
- Diver qualifications.
- Dive medicals.
- Dive planning.
- Equipment.
- Dive procedures shore dive.
- Dive procedures boat dive.
- Night dive.
- Deep dive.
- Wreck dive.
- Cavern dive.
- Altitude dive.
- Cold water dive.
- Repetitive dive.
- Solo dive.
- Dive tables.
- Emergency procedures.
- First aid and resuscitation.
- Diver rescue procedure.

Procedure Review Trigger

The trigger for the procedure review can be from any of the following sources:

- Diver complaints.
- Dive log.
- Incident reports.
- Dive SOPs audit.

Dive Procedure Review Process

The review process involves looking at the problematic procedure and the situation (conditions, activity, and diver capability). Identify the problem(s) it causes. These can then be investigated through cause analysis to determine risk mitigation that can be used to update procedures. The dive procedure review process is shown at Figure 14.6.

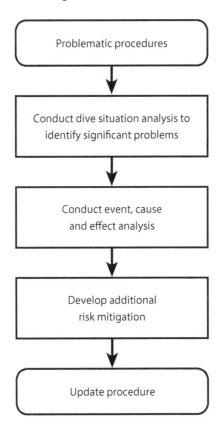

Figure 14.6. Procedure review process

Annex II
POST DIVE INCIDENT OR NEAR MISS

Introduction

Following a dive incident or a near miss there is a need to determine the cause so that on future dives it is not repeated. If an incident or near miss is ignored, in the future a repetition could possibly lead to an *accident* (serious damage, injury or fatality). Diving accidents are investigated by authorised professionals such as police, coastguards, coroners, etc.

On completion of this annex, you should be able to produce a dive related incident/near miss investigation report.

Dive Incident Report

An Incident Report is an important document. If one is completed, it should outline the conditions surrounding what has happened, such as:

- Details of diver(s) involved.
- Date, time and location.
- Type and description of incident.
- Details of person making report.

This report should be made as soon as practicable (preferably contemporaneously with the incident) following the dive incident. In any situation where two or more people confer to enable a report this should be made clear to avoid suggestions of improper or hidden 'collusion'.

Investigation Steps

The investigation process follows several sequential steps to identify the true cause of the incident, as follows:

- Gather evidence.
- Determine the time and location during the dive activity when the incident occurred.
- Determine the conditions during the dive activity when the incident occurred.
- Determine what happened (the event).
- Determine the cause(s) of the event.

Witnesses

Persons that witnessed the incident or were in the vicinity should be interviewed. This is likely to include dive buddies and/or other members of the dive team.

Evidence and Sources

The investigation focuses on the cause(s) of the incident. If a report is available, the risk can be established, which then leads to determining the cause(s) of the incident.

The incident causation categories, sub-categories and source of evidence to determine the cause(s) involved are shown at Table 14.7.

Incident Causation Categories	Incident Causation Sub-Categories	Source of Evidence
Fitness of diver	• Medical fitness • Psychological fitness • Physical fitness	• Medical record • Self-declaration
Qualification of diver	• Qualification appropriate for specific dive	• Qualification record
Experience of diver	• Experience appropriate for specific dive	• Personal dive log • Self-declaration
Conditions	• Surface conditions • Underwater conditions	• Team dive log
Equipment	• Appropriateness for specific dive • Serviceability of equipment	• Investigation of equipment • Maintenance record
Dive procedures	• Suitability for dive • Adherence to procedures	• Standard operating procedures • Dive plan
Interaction with marine life	• Hazardous marine life	• Dive plan • Incident report
Safety equipment	• Appropriateness for specific dive	• Investigation of safety equipment • Standard operating procedures
Rescue capability	• Appropriateness for specific dive	• Standard operating procedures • Dive plan
Medical evacuation capability	• Appropriateness for specific dive location	• Standard operating procedures • Dive plan
Water entry/exit methodology	• Appropriateness for specific dive	• Standard operating procedures • Dive plan

Table 14.7. Causation investigation evidence source

Incident or Near Miss Investigation Process

The investigation process involves gathering the evidence and using analysis tools. The steps are shown at Figure 14.8.

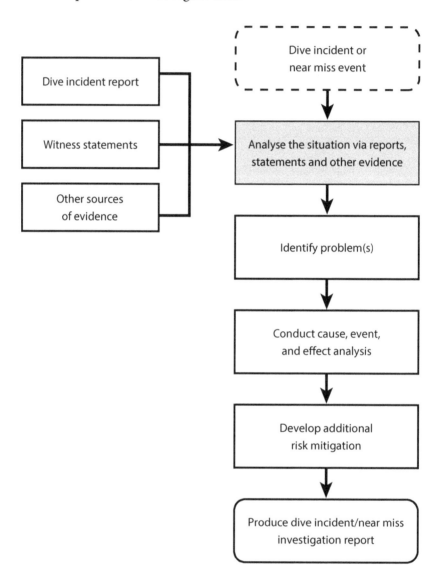

Figure 14.8. Dive incident investigation process

Annex III
TASK FAILURE

Introduction

A dive activity may have failed to achieve a satisfactory task outcome. The failure is the result of problems that may have occurred during the task execution phase(s). Risk management can be used to walk back through the phases and identify critical failure points.

On completion of this annex, you should be able to conduct a task failure investigation.

Analysis

Task failure investigation involves analysis of the dive situation (conditions, dive activity and diver capability) and the task phases to identify the problems that prevented the task being completed.

Situation Analysis

The elements that contribute to the execution of the dive and task are analysed to determine:

- Dive conditions, activity, and diver capability.
- Method for performing the task.
- Task phases.
- Duties of each diver in performing the task.
- Equipment required for performing the task.
- Causes relating to performance of the task.
- Time allocated to perform the task.
- Location of the task.
- Accessibility to the task location.

Task Phase Analysis

Task phase analysis is the breakdown of the task into phases and the analysis of each phase to identify potential failures/problems. An analysis matrix associated with a lost item search and recovery is shown at Table 14.9.

Task Phases	Potential Failure/Problem
Establish circular search	• Unable to determine approximate location of lost outboard motor
Conduct circular search	• Unable to locate outboard motor
Marking location of lost outboard motor	• Unable to mark location of outboard motor
Swim lift bag to location of lost outboard motor	• Cannot relocate outboard motor position
Attach lift bags to outboard motor	• Unable to attach lift bag to outboard motor
Inflate lift bag	• Unable to inflate lift bag
Follow lift bags and outboard motor to surface	• Lose control of lift bag and outboard motor during ascent • Outboard motor detaches from lift bag during ascent • Diver gets entangled with lift bag during ascent
Recovery of outboard motor onto boat	• Unable to recover outboard motor onto boat

Table 14.9. Task and failure identification

Task Investigation Process

Once the failure/problem has been identified, risk management can be used to identify the risk (cause, event and effect) and develop controls. The steps of the investigation process are shown at Figure 14.10.

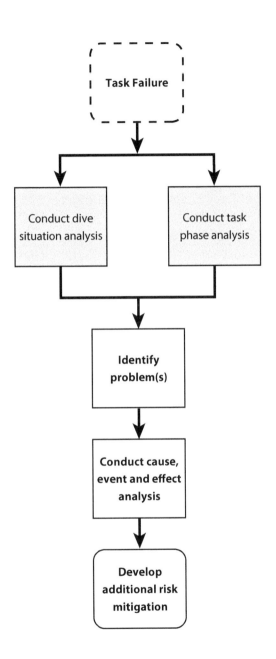

Figure 14.10. Task investigation process

Annex IV
DIVE EQUIPMENT FAILURE

Introduction

During a dive, an equipment failure may be experienced which results in a near miss or incident. In these circumstances the failure needs to be investigated to prevent an event which could lead to a serious or fatal accident.

On completion of this annex, you should be able to conduct a dive equipment failure investigation.

Equipment Source of Information

Reference to manufacturers' manuals should indicate the suitability and limitations of individual items of dive equipment.

Situation Analysis

A failure of dive equipment may result from the following situations:

- Conditions in which equipment is being used.
- Activity conducted.
- Diver capability to use the equipment.
- Procedure for use of equipment.
- Serviceability of equipment.
- Suitability of equipment.

Problem Investigation Matrix

The equipment investigation is conducted using a matrix to narrow the focus on the key problem, as shown at Table 14.11.

Equipment Investigation Process

The overall investigation process to determine the problem(s) is shown at Figure 14.12.

Equipment category	Equipment sub-category	Situation category	Situation sub-category	Issues contributing to problem
Time/depth monitoring	Dive computer	Conditions	Cold water	Diver wearing gloves
		Activity	Recreational dive	No problem
		Diver capability	Advanced Open Water	No problem
		Procedures	Acceptable	Diver unable to manipulate buttons
		Serviceability	Serviceable	No problem
		Suitability	Unsuitable	Buttons too small for gloved operation

Table 14.11. Investigation matrix

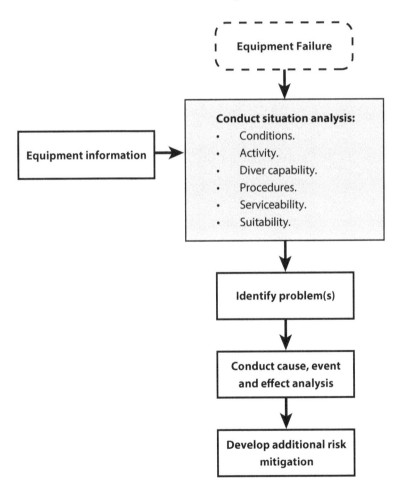

Figure 14.12. Equipment investigation process

Chapter 15

RISK MONITOR AND REVIEW

Introduction

Risk monitoring and review are cyclical processes for overseeing the execution of dives over a period of time which may be a single or multiple days. They are programmed actions in response to changing situations and should not be confused with the risk investigation which is in response to failures, near misses or incidents (as discussed in Chapter 14).

This chapter explains how monitoring and review techniques are used to identify and manage dive problems as they emerge during the dive and are reported by divers following one or more dives.

On completion of this chapter, you should be able to monitor situational parameters during dive activities and conduct periodic risk reviews.

The Changing Dive Situation

Over any period of successive diving, the situation can change to the point where diving may become dangerous. Consequently, the situation requires continuous monitoring and periodic review to ensure risk mitigation is still valid. Situational factors requiring monitoring and review are as follows:

- Conditions — these can change very rapidly during the day.
- Diving activities and tasks — these may appear feasible during planning but in practice turn out to be challenging.
- Diver capability — this may be overestimated during planning resulting in divers getting tired or overwhelmed during dives.

Dive Risk Monitoring

This is the continuous observation and supervision over the day's diving activities. The aim is to detect changes which may affect the safety and outcome of each dive. As significant differences in the situation are identified, immediate risk assessments are implemented in situ and quick decisions are arrived at as to whether to continue the dive activity or abort/cancel pending a detailed review.

Dive Risk Review

This is a process of periodically reassessing the effectiveness of existing risk mitigation and the identification of new risks that may emerge during dive activities. This can be performed as often as required, for example at the end of each day of diving or at the end of each week of diving. The risk review involves a detailed analysis of problematic risk mitigation and management of any new risks.

To assist with the review a checklist can be used to systematically work through the process and record problems identified in each phase of the activity. Suggested mitigation can be noted for further investigation. An example is shown at Table 15.1 and a template is provided at Table 15.2.

Exercise — Risk Review

Conduct a review of multiple dives carried out over a period and determine if the rules or mitigation that you defined at the beginning continued to remain valid to the end. Enter a summary of your review in the Risk Register.

Activity	Identified Problems	Suggested Mitigation
Loading dive boat	Boat noted listing dangerously to starboard during sea passage to dive site	Dive officer/supervisor to ensure dive equipment loaded onboard is evenly distributed
Sea passage to dive site	Diver fell overboard during sea passage to dive site	Predive briefing to include action for person overboard during sea passage
Dressing for the dive	Some divers noted getting entangled in scuba harness during donning process	Buddy divers to assist each other during dressing. Dive supervisor to monitor activity.
Water entry from boat	Divers noted entering water with equipment missing, e.g. weight belt, fins, computer, etc.	Buddy divers to check each other prior to water entry. Dive brief to emphasise buddy checks and to control eagerness to be the first in the water.
Descent to bottom	Diver noted unable to control rapid descent as low pressure hose to buoyancy compensator not connected, resulting in severe ear squeeze	Buddy divers to check each other prior to water entry. Dive brief to emphasise buddy checks and to control eagerness to be the first in the water.
Activity on bottom	Diver noticed air leak from buddy's regulator first stage half-way through dive, necessitating premature termination	Buddy divers to conduct bubble check immediately after water entry, at 5 metres depth
Ascent to surface	Diver experienced joint pains shortly after surfacing from second dive of the day to 30 metres depth	Pre-dive briefing to emphasise importance of safety stops and commencement of ascent from bottom one to two minutes prior to reaching limit of no-decompression bottom time. Also consider extending surface interval between first and second deep dive.
Water exit to boat	Diver fell off boat ladder and landed on diver below during exit from water	Divers to remove fins prior to climbing boat ladder. Other divers to stay away from ladder until preceding diver is on board the boat.
Post dive activity	During sea passage back to port equipment noted rolling around the deck, smashing into boat structure and other equipment	Diving supervisor to ensure all equipment is stowed correctly prior to lifting anchor. Immediate post dive briefing should cover this issue.

Table 15.1. Boat dive review checklist example

MONITOR AND REVIEW

BOAT DIVE RISK REVIEW TEMPLATE

Download this template from:
www.DivedUp.com/diving-risk-management-templates/

Activity	Identified Problems	Suggested Mitigation
Loading dive boat		
Sea passage to dive site		
Dressing for the dive		
Water entry from boat		
Descent to bottom		
Activity on bottom		
Ascent to surface		
Water exit to boat		
Post dive activity		

Table 15.2. Boat dive review template

Final Thoughts

Risk is a constant factor in any adventurous activity. Helpfully, diving is now highly evolved with a generally very good safety record. However, adverse events do and will still occur. By remembering to consider the advice in this book, it is hoped you can identify more of these events before they happen, mitigate against them, and continue enjoying diving without major incident. With that in mind, stay alert, stay safe and have fun.

About the Author

Claudio Gino Ferreri BSc (Security) has made risk management his life's work, having dived as a member of the Australian SAS, been a permanent acting police senior sergeant with the Western Australia counter-terrorism and bomb disposal teams, and a government security manager for the Anti Corruption Commission and the Corruption and Crime Commission. He holds recreational diving qualifications to TDI Trimix level, and has served as committee member and Diving Officer to the Underwater Explorers Club of Western Australia.

Acknowledgements

Initially, I wish to acknowledge and thank my dear wife Pauline for her support. Over many decades, during my frequent absences from home, she raised our two children, managed the home and pursued a career as a neonatal nurse. Her physical and emotional support not only enabled me to follow my vocations but ultimately lead me to writing this book.

Secondly, I need to acknowledge the countless number of unconventional free thinking individuals in Australia and abroad who over many decades provided me with the knowledge, skill and experience which was so essential for the rationale behind the formulation of this book. They know who they are. I do not need to mention their names.

Finally, I want to acknowledge Alex Gibson, Dived Up Editor-in-Chief for his support and expertise in transforming my manuscript into a polished and commercially viable book.

List of Figures and Tables

Index

DIVING EQUIPMENT
CHOICE, MAINTENANCE AND FUNCTION
by Jonas Arvidsson

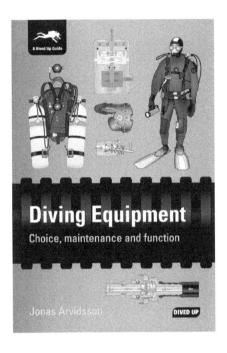

'Extremely well-researched, well-written and comprehensive…
should be on every diver's bookshelf.'— *Divernet*

'First thing I have to say about this book is that every sports diver should
have one… Diving gear is not cheap and can become a serious investment,
so knowing what to choose and how best to ensure its long and reliable
life is to my mind definitely worth the cost of this book.'— *Scubaverse*

Paperback and Ebook | ISBN 978-1-909455-13-9

www.DivedUp.com

DIVING THE THISTLEGORM
THE ULTIMATE GUIDE TO A WORLD WAR II SHIPWRECK
by Simon Brown, Jon Henderson, Alex Mustard and Mike Postons
Foreword by Emad Khalil

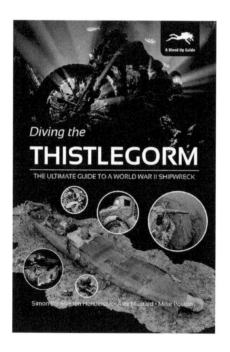

'There's so much to admire here ... I recommend this superb book.'— *SCUBA*

'A brilliant in depth guide to the wreck and all it's facets, all illustrated by superb photos and graphics.'— *Scubaverse*

'The most comprehensive guide to one of the world's greatest shipwrecks'— *Emad Khalil, Alexandria University (from the Foreword)*

Hardback, Paperback and Ebook | ISBN 978-1-909455-37-5

www.DivedUp.com